Charleston · City of Gardens

Charleston

CITY OF GARDENS

LOUISA PRINGLE CAMERON

Foreword by the Honorable Joseph P. Riley Jr.

THE UNIVERSITY OF SOUTH CAROLINA PRESS

Published by the University of South Carolina Press
Columbia, South Carolina 29208

www.sc.edu/uscpress

Manufactured in China

27 26 25 24 23 22 21 20 19 18
10 9 8 7 6 5 4 3 2 1

Library of Congress Cataloging-in-Publication Data
can be found at http://catalog.loc.gov/.

ISBN: 978-1-61117-818-0 (cloth)
ISBN: 978-1-61117-819-7 (ebook)

FRONTISPIECE A view through a gate on Meeting Street. Espaliered evergreens, grapevine, and a hanging basket of begonias help soften the high brick walls to the left that have a northern exposure.

This book is lovingly dedicated to my husband of forty years, Price Cameron. His skills as a plastic surgeon have been redirected to the garden, where he is happily painting trompe l'oeil works of art on the walls and continuing to tweak the design and planting of his overall plan. I heartily thank him not only for his patience but also for all of his good advice and delicious meals.

Trompe l'oeil tondi from the works of della Robbia, by Price Cameron

Contents

Foreword

When someone I've met while visiting another city asks me, "What is Charleston like?," my answer is, "It is America's most beautiful city." That is not mayoral prideful exaggeration—it is the truth; there is no city in America like it. This city's beauty is the sum total of its so many exquisite parts: gorgeous buildings large and small, the pastel palette of its historic stucco homes, the human scale of the city, its architecture, the detail of the ensemble of its eighteenth- and nineteenth-century buildings, and what is often underrecognized: its exquisite parks and gardens. In Louisa Pringle Cameron's *Charleston: City of Gardens,* we come to understand better the role Charleston's gardens have in creating this most beautiful city.

The job of mayor, which the citizens of Charleston were so gracious to bestow on me for a substantial period, allowed me so many pleasures. None has been greater than the opportunity to work with our dedicated parks department, its staff, and the skilled landscape architects and designers to create new parks and to give rebirth to somewhat forgotten, forlorn, or underused older parks.

The site of the waterfront park was for centuries used for shipping. Wharfs, piers, and terminals occupied this space until a horrific fire in 1955. The site then languished for almost a generation and what remained was charred pilings and a large rubble-filled parking lot. In the late 1970s a developer acquired it with plans to build a commercial project. I, newly elected, and with the support of two most wonderful citizens, Charles and Betty Woodward, was convinced that what a great city would do was use that land for a public park and give the water's edge and its remarkable vista to our citizens forever. Once acquiring the land, we assembled a world-class team of landscape architects, architects, planners, and designers to create a beautiful waterfront park worthy of this city. When the team arrived in Charleston, I told them all to put their pencils and sketchpads aside, as we were going to take a walk. What I wanted was for the designers, rather than following any preconceived notions of what the park should be, to first come to understand this amazing city. We started on Chalmers Street, walked through the Confederate Home's surprising garden, and then wandered up and down the narrow streets and cobblestone and bluestone alleys winding through the Historic District. We peeked into dozens of gardens: I took them to Mrs. Whaley's garden, then down Church Street and along the Battery to White Point Gardens, and then down lower King Street, Legare Street, and much more, peering and peeking all the while. It did take about four hours, and Louisa mentions Stu Dawson referred to it as "*a forced march*." When the walk was over, the designers, now exposed to and inspired by the scale and the beauty of the city and its gardens, had begun to learn the design language of Charleston so that we could then commence together to design the park. It was important that the park, when finished—as well as now, twenty-seven years later—would feel like a natural part of Charleston and of its many lovely parks and gardens.

In my forty years as mayor, the city built eighty-six new parks and restored forty-two existing parks. When the city annexed the five thousand acres that is Daniel Island, the owners asked what the city's commitment would be to help develop the property; our answer was a series of parks. The owners expected our response would be about the highways and infrastructure, but what I told the owners was what would define Daniel Island would be the parks system. It now of course has become a wonderful place for people to live and work and is still growing, but what makes it remarkable is the system of large and small parks, each different, all beautiful, and loved.

We build large parks and, just as important, small parks. Two special, almost tiny parks among those are the Charlotte Street Park with the Irish Memorial along the harbor at the end of Charlotte Street, which commands a most wonderful vista of the harbor and allows the park visitor to step down very close to the water's edge, and our newest achievement, Theodora Park, at Anson and George Street, the brainchild of one of our great citizens, David Rawle, that honors his mother, Theodora Rawle, and has the same restorative powers that Paley Park has in bustling New York City.

You will want to keep this book nearby on a coffee table or a favorite shelf on a bookcase. If you're a visitor, you will later pick it up to fill you with warm reminders of this city of beautiful gardens, and then resolve to return as soon as you can. And if you're fortunate enough to live in the lowcountry, you will pick it up and vow to explore the treasures of *Charleston: City of Gardens* often.

JOSEPH P. RILEY JR.

Acknowledgments

I am profoundly grateful to each and every gardener represented in this book for making this work possible. I could not begin to write about these wonderful gardens without their generosity with time and knowledge, as well as their willingness to open their gates.

I am deeply grateful to my kind and patient editor, Jonathan Haupt, director of the University of South Carolina Press, for his gentle encouragement and his delicate and tactful handling of my many, many questions. Susan Epstein gave most helpful input. The design and production manager at the press, Pat Callahan, exercised great patience with my technical issues; Elizabeth Farry worked hard straightening out my problems with Word; and the Press intern Stephanie Sarkany did a wonderful job proofreading and standardizing my work.

The staffs at the Charleston County Library, the City of Charleston's Horticultural Departments, and the Charleston County RMC office, and Karen Emmons, archivist for Historic Charleston Foundation, were not only helpful; they were cheerful and enthusiastic about this project as well. Finally, my insightful friend Maurice Thompson gave generously of her time to proofread. Thank you all so very much.

I would like for my readers to understand that I am not a professional photographer, but I hope that the images in this book will illustrate the beauty, style, and interest of these lovely spaces that we call gardens. I also hope that the photographs will inspire readers to try new ideas of their own.

Plant Nomenclature

Any mistakes in the plant nomenclature throughout this book are my responsibility. I used *Hortus Third* as the final authority. It was last published in 1976 by the Liberty Hyde Bailey Hortorium, and there have been reclassifications, corrections, new introductions, and so on since then.

In *Hortus,* the family names are given first (example: *Liliaceae* and *Rosaceae*) but are not generally used when describing plants. There is also a category for form names, which are given for sporadic or minor variations, but it is not often used except in horticulture. An × is the sign for a hybrid, which is the result of crossing two plants belonging to different species or varieties or by crossing two plants belonging to distinct forms of the same species or variety.

The common names of plants are generally not capitalized in writing. One more note: In botanical description there is an exception to the rule that requires placing closing punctuation within quotation marks.

The Latin names of plants are written in the following basic order and grammar:

Genus	The name is always Capitalized and either *italicized* or <u>underlined</u>.
species	The name is always lowercase and either *italicized* or <u>underlined</u>.
variety	A variety is a natural mutation. It is sometimes denoted by the abbreviation var. followed by the name of the variety. It is never capitalized unless it is a proper name.
'Cultivar'	A cultivar is a mutation that occurs as a result of human influence. The cultivar name is always capitalized, never italicized or underlined, and it is either set off by single quotation marks or preceded by the abbreviation cv.

Example: I would like to order an *Acer palmatum* dissectum 'Viridis'.

This name describes a deciduous green lace-leaf Japanese maple with specific characteristics. *Acer* is the generic term for maple; *palmatum* means the leaves have five or more veins arising from a point or are palmlike; dissectum means deeply cut or divided into segments; and 'Viridis' is the Latin word for green.

INTRODUCTION

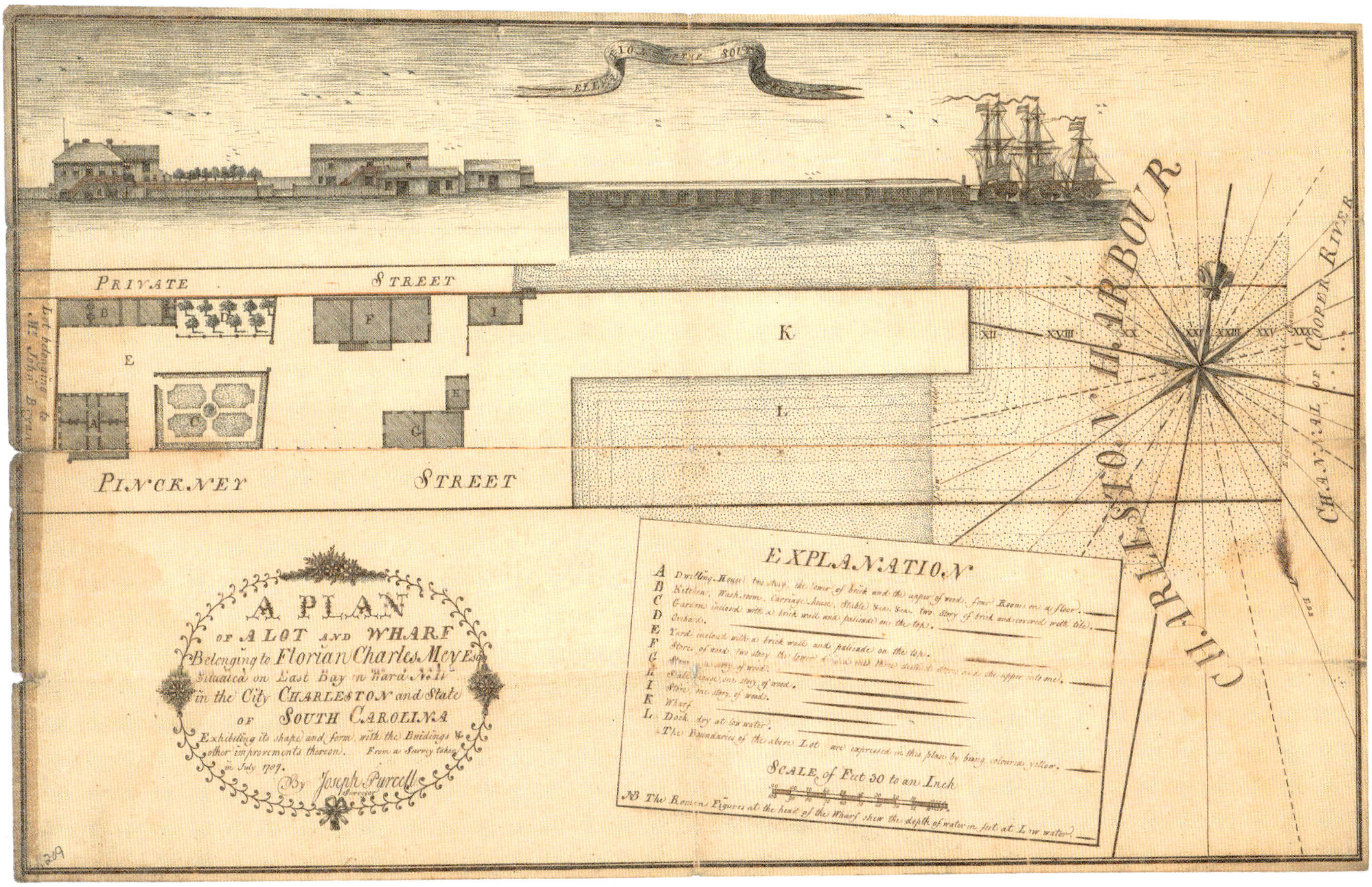

Early city plats showing gardens are rare. Charlie Lybrand at the Charleston County Register of Mesne Conveyance and Walt Dunlap, a dedicated volunteer, have spent years scanning old maps and plats, the earliest of which currently dates back to 1706. This is a fine example.

SO MUCH HAS BEEN WRITTEN about the gardens of Charleston, both private and public, that it would seem another book about them would be repetitious. Happily, such is not the case. Gardens can be dynamic, ephemeral, extremely diverse, and very personal. Every year exciting new plant material is introduced, often with fanfare, providing a delicious array of choices. As in the world of design, the newest materials are soon in fashion and, conversely, that which was recently considered old-fashioned again becomes the latest rage. The now frequent turnover of real estate in Charleston results in constant reinterpretations of properties: new gardeners move in and old plantings are moved out; a landscape architect or designer is consulted;

play areas are removed or installed; a garage is built or perhaps torn down for more space; newly erected walls provide vertical gardening surfaces or privacy; pools are filled in, reworked, or installed; and on it goes. Even established gardens need refurbishing, rescaling, and frequent replacements. As an example, plans are underway for work on the garden of one of the most beautiful and important houses on the East Coast: the Miles Brewton House on King Street. This stunning example of Georgian architecture was once on a larger lot, but it still retains a good-sized garden behind the mansion. In his book on Mary Pringle, who lived at the Miles Brewton House, the author Richard N. Côté describes the yard and garden:

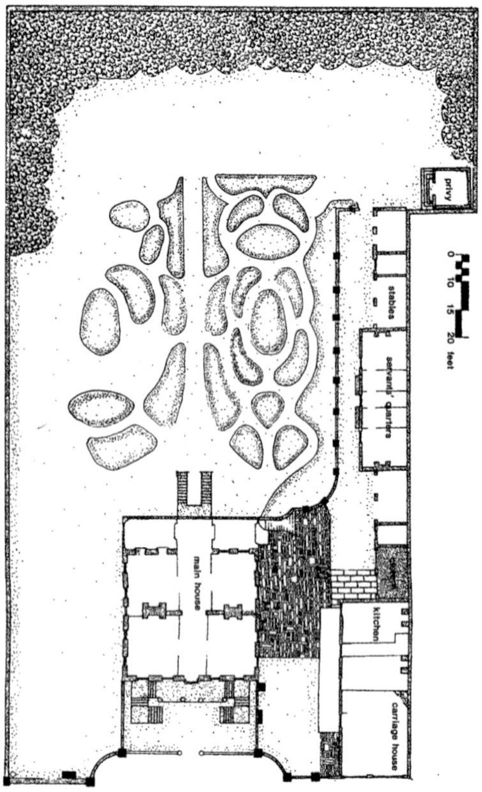

Plan of the Miles Brewton House. Courtesy of the Register Mesne Conveyance, Charleston County, South Carolina

> The original site plan for the Miles Brewton House included outbuildings containing a twin-bay coach house, stalls, a kitchen, a privy and living quarters for the servants. There were six double-tie stalls, adequate for the cows, the matched teams of coach horses, several riding horses for family use, and those of overnight visitors. Two tack rooms and a harness room were required for housing and maintaining the harnesses and the harness room may also have served as residence for the coachman and his family. The kitchen complex included a large cistern for storing water and a spacious baking oven. The entire back yard, extending all the way to Legaré Street, was at one time a formal garden in the English style. Jacob Motte Alston noted that in antebellum times, an English gardener "kept all in perfect order, and supplied all the vegetables of the season." The broad walks were lined with sea shells, and mockingbirds and cardinals nested throughout. The snowdrops in the garden in the 1930s were believed to be the same brought by Miles Brewton from England, and the garden was the beneficiary of seeds and cuttings from Edward Pringle in California, Julius Pringle in France, and friends and relatives throughout the lowcountry. In spring and early summer the garden was a riot of colors and fragrances from Bermuda lilies, jonquils, sweet olives, lilacs, Cape Jessamine, oleander, English violets, pinks, carnations and a variety of roses. The garden also produced fruits and vegetables for the family, including oranges, pears, figs, peaches, grapes, pomegranates, bananas, French artichokes and corn. To the rear of the garden is one of the two original outhouses. Other buildings in the yard included coops and pens for the children's guinea pigs, rabbits, squirrels, cranes, and other birds and animals.
>
> Richard N. Côté, *Mary's World* (2001)

In my previous two books, I wrote only about and photographed gardens on the Lower Peninsula, with a few exceptions. *The Private Gardens of Charleston* was my first attempt to describe the personal creations of a talented group of gardeners, landscape architects, designers, and craftsmen within the challenging confines of the downtown Historic District. Hurricane Hugo changed the landscape forever in 1989, and *The Secret Gardens of*

Charleston addressed the valiant efforts made to restore order in the years following that devastating storm.

In this volume I hope to give the reader an idea of the enormous scope of gardening in the city of Charleston, including areas beyond the Lower Peninsula. Visitors are always eager for glimpses of the exquisite private gardens surrounding historic properties, but there are many other inviting residential gardens and lovely parks, as well as handsome museum gardens, institutional gardens, cemeteries, graveyards, and public spaces maintained by city staff and volunteers. Our moderate climate, lengthy growing season, and generous annual rainfall allow thousands of species of plants and trees to thrive. Even certain tropical plants flourish in protected locations.

The history of horticulture in the lowcountry, and specifically in Charleston, is a long one. At Charles Towne Landing, situated on the banks of the Ashley River a few miles northwest of the peninsula, the state has recreated a portion of the original settlement of Charleston in 1670, including a garden of food crops, experimental plants, and ornamentals. By 1680 the settlement had moved to the peninsula, and residents were building houses and gardens. Newspapers from the early 1700s include notices advertising the services of several persons for designing and laying out kitchen and pleasure gardens. Famous early botanists, artists, and explorers who left their imprint in the libraries and on the landscape include Mark Catesby, André Michaux, Alexander Garden, John Bartram, Thomas Walter, Joel Poinsett, and John James Audubon. The Charleston Museum published *A Gardener's Kalendar* from the original 1756 almanac that gives "Directions for managing a Kitchen-Garden every Month in the Year. Done by a Lady." The 1810 catalogue of the Botanik Garden of South Carolina in Charleston lists 494 plants and their origins. Other historic papers provide descriptions of a large variety of crops and flower gardens on plantations and all over the city. Seed merchants and nurserymen traded far afield, and there was a lively exchange with Great Britain and France. The first rose hybridized in America was grown at a farm just south of Charleston and was the start of the Noisette classification of roses.

Because of fires, floods, wars, hurricanes, development, and personal taste, no early city gardens remain, but two or three small "pattern" gardens from the nineteenth century have been carefully preserved. Several of the twentieth-century gardens planned by Loutrel Briggs, the landscape architect whose designs are synonymous with the term *Charleston Gardens,* have been renovated. An important garden on Legare Street was meticulously restored to its nearly original nineteenth-century appearance. Several gardens mentioned as newly planted in *The Private Gardens of Charleston* and *The Secret Gardens of Charleston* have matured beautifully, and it is a pleasure to see them as their designers and caretakers envisioned. New gardens are thriving in the oldest sections of the city. There are stunning examples attached to fine houses on Broad, Church, King, Meeting, Chalmers, and Archdale Streets. Then there are a few less-dressed-up gardens that retain an air of mystery and romance through benign neglect. Beautifully wrought ironwork and old brick walls, as well as handsome wooden gates and fences, are all hallmarks of the "Charleston Garden." Old and new, manicured and shabby, mostly green or very gaudy, there are no two gardens alike.

The "Big Three" gardens not far from the city—Middleton Place, Magnolia Gardens, and Cypress Gardens—have drawn visitors from all over the world for decades, and each offers a different experience in addition to acres of superb gardens and year-round bloom. Middleton has an eighteenth-century museum house, Magnolia features a petting zoo for children, and Cypress is home to a butterfly greenhouse. Brookgreen Gardens, featuring a superb collection of American outdoor sculpture set in extensive gardens, is seventy miles north of Charleston.

Green space has become a popular concept over the past decade or two, and the City of Charleston has made great strides toward improving and maintaining its public parks. In addition the recently organized Charleston Parks Conservancy has rallied citizen support for all the parks and works closely with the city. The Charleston Horticultural Society was founded just over a decade ago. Its mission is to "promote horticultural excellence in the lowcountry," and it provides a multitude of resources and educational programs on a year-round basis. One offering includes a map of the Heritage Rose Trail and a brochure describing old roses in churchyards and other historic locations on the peninsula. In addition to the work of these organizations, the Garden Club of Charleston maintains gardens for the Charleston Museum, as well as the plantings along the Gateway Walk located in the center of the old city. Historic Charleston Foundation and the Preservation Society of Charleston continue to sponsor annual tours of private houses and gardens that are wildly popular. Brilliant lecturers, garden experts, and authors all contribute to the events taking place during the weeks of these tours. Both the College of Charleston and Ashley Hall School not only have beautiful grounds, but they also raise funds through garden tours, as do various alumni groups and garden clubs. The Medical University of South Carolina has three gardens worth visiting; one of them is an extensive vegetable garden right on campus. Roper St. Francis Hospital has a meditation garden at their West Ashley location featuring a labyrinth, a particularly magnificent live oak tree, sculpture, architectural gates, a fountain, and many benches for contemplating the roses and shade plantings.

The talented and dedicated landscape architects, landscape designers, horticulturalists, and nurserymen in the area have played a major part in the evolution of the city's gardens, often giving generously of their time and resources to help with numerous and varied projects. Volunteers and volunteer organizations, including the Tri-County Master Gardeners, give their time to help maintain public and semipublic spaces. One nursery annually invites Horticultural Society members to visit its wholesale greenhouses, tour the plantings on the grounds, and purchase plants at retail. The Native Plant

Society, the Camellia Society, and other similar groups conduct meetings, workshops, and shows in the area and are superb sources of information in addition to all the local retail nurseries.

I hope that this book will leave the reader with a sense that the gardening history of Charleston is still very much in the making. Text and photographs alone cannot do justice to the actual experience of being in a Charleston garden with its visual and tactile feasts, gentle sounds of running water and birdsong and sweet fragrances. These gardens are very much an integral part of the visual arts of the city, along with its architecture, art, theater, dance, and music. They are a treasure.

A view of the College of Charleston's main campus

25

PRIVATE GARDENS

ALTHOUGH WE HAVE A WEALTH of domestic architecture in the city, from simple freeman's homes to grand mansions and some good modern buildings, garden space on the peninsula is usually quite limited. There are lots of walls and neighbors' windows and fences to consider when landscaping, as well as sidewalk landscapes and access alleys. Sometimes the only path to the garden is through the house. All of these things, as well as the fact that the gardens often literally become a part of the property's living space, factor into making Charleston a city of some of the most charming and individual gardens in the world. Simply put, no two are alike.

If you are out on a stroll, take note of the enormous variety of patterns, old and modern, in the gates, espalier designs, fences, water features, brickwork, drive and walkway treatments using plants and hardscape materials, the statuary, the use of trees, the shaping of shrubbery, and the placement of hundreds and hundreds of pots, unusual containers, and window boxes. We are fortunate to have a mild climate that allows gardeners to experiment with a huge range of plant material that does not usually have to be winterized. Our gardens are in bloom all year long and we take great pride in them.

Courtyard Gardens

THE COURTYARD GARDEN OF THE WILLIAM ELLIOTT HOUSE (CA. 1739)

The garden of one of the oldest single houses in the city has undergone multiple transformations in the past few decades. When Kenneth and Monica Seeger bought the house in 2010, the area outside the house and its attached kitchen building was planted with specimen trees in boxwood parterres and was quite shady. The previous owner's hobby was a tree plantation and nursery. Charleston's much-loved landscape architect of the mid-twentieth century, Loutrel Briggs, had left his mark on the property, too.

FACING Colorful pots of purple-heart (*Tradescantia pallida*), begonias, impatiens, and roses enhance an eighteenth-century house on Queen Street.

There is no lawn at the William Elliott House garden, and the flower beds are instead set off by a variety of stones and bricks in different designs and patterns.

Monica Seeger, a knowledgeable and talented gardener, had never had a southern garden and was excited by the potential of the small, confined space. She hired Sheila Wertimer to help redesign the courtyard and give advice on plant material. "I didn't want to change the basic layout; it was important to me that the garden worked with the old house and looked like it had been there for many years," she explained. "I also wanted several seating areas for entertaining, as well as a comfortable place just to enjoy the garden and listen to the church bells."

A Persian ironwood tree (*Parrottia persica*) was carefully moved to its new location against the back wall, other trees were limbed up, the fountain was rebuilt, and dozens of camellias, sasanquas, hydrangeas, plumbagos, hostas, ferns, and flax lilies were planted.

A changing assortment of shrubs, bulbs, annuals, and perennials fills the parterres.

There are dozens of urns and pots that hold interesting foliage plants and colorful arrangements. Many of the pots were gifts and serve as reminders of friends and distant places. A goat cart sits near the front door that Mrs. Seeger particularly enjoys decorating for the holidays and the four seasons. David Dozier, a local landscape architect, is a tremendous help with the garden maintenance and with ideas for new plant combinations. The driveway is kept fairly simple, using mainly green and white textured plants in the narrow beds with sasanquas espaliered against the pale wall.

There is no lawn to maintain, but in a sunny spot just beyond the front porch, there are four boxwood parterres filled with perennials and annuals that require constant attention. A low iron fence and a gate with an arch divide this area from a terrace at the back. This is the largest area of the garden and has seating at its southern semicircular end, a fountain and pool, and a table and chairs at the northern end against the kitchen house. The kitchen house has supports for the pale yellow-white 'Sally Holmes' rose that is being trained up and over the windows.

A well-pruned oak tree spreads its branches over half of this back courtyard paved with flagstone, providing filtered shade for the hydrangeas and other shade plants below. High up in the tall brick wall that defines one of the property lines, a pittosporum shrub took root sometime in the past. It looks like an ancient bonsai or something out of Angkor Wat and lends an air of mystery to the spot.

The wrought-iron gate to the driveway on the left of the house allows passersby to glimpse the garden. "I am passionate about creating beauty through gardening," says Mrs. Seeger, "and I knew that I was in a place where not only could I accomplish this, but also where it would be appreciated. I want people to walk by and smile."

Colorful planters decorate the driveway gates of the courtyard.

A PIED-À-TERRE COURTYARD

It has taken more than three years to perfect this garden room. When Paul and Paula Thomas finally found their perfect pied-à-terre in part of the mid-nineteenth-century Dowd Tenements, they approached its renovation slowly and carefully, using as many original materials as possible.

In the fifteen-by-sixteen-foot courtyard that served as the entrance to their home, they removed broken brick paving, laid down handsome flagstones, and took out the lone tree in the corner: an overgrown holly bush that served as an evening roost for city doves. Eliminating a lattice gate and screen further opened the space.

Clay Richardson, a talented carpenter, fashioned a new gate and a mahogany receptacle for the city-issued garbage can. The copper surface works well as an outdoor counter top.

Keeping everything in the proper scale was important to the couple, as were other elements of design. Repetition, texture, color, balance, and atmosphere are all part of the scheme. A ribbon palm, not often seen in the city, was installed in the corner where the holly formerly gave too much shade. This particular palm tree's fronds make lovely sounds when the wind blows. The sound and sight of water is important, too. A lead cistern, made in England, adds the right touch.

The pièce de résistance, however, is the Veneman patio furniture. The design is based on eighteenth-century French patterns, but the color is modern and fun. The Thomases "wanted the space to blend in and not be at odds with old Charleston and yet be uniquely ours." *Res ipsa loquitur.*

Veneman outdoor furniture
brightens up the courtyard.

AN ANSONBOROUGH COURTYARD

Twenty years ago, Dr. J. Gilbert and Constance Baldwin bought a house in Ansonborough with a courtyard garden that had already been well landscaped by previous owners. The twenty-one-by-thirty-five-foot space was dominated by brick walls and a neighboring three-story old brick house with tall brick chimneys. Successfully, the focus of the area was from eye level down, with a triple fountain, a small pool, and a patch of lawn.

When the couple renovated the kitchen in the back of the house, they added a sunlit passage with triple French doors opening into the courtyard, embracing the space as if it were another room, but the lawn "carpet" became a high-maintenance feature. "It took longer to get the mower out from storage than to run it over the lawn, " laughs Dr. Baldwin, "and we had to replace the St. Augustine sod at least four or five times. We either over- or underwatered every year."

Pots of herbs fill a corner below several stories of brick at the entrance to the garden through the driveway.

The solution surprised everyone. A close friend who is an expert gardener remarked that he could solve the problem for one thousand dollars, and the next day he was presented with a check for that amount. Soon (and more than one thousand dollars later), gravel replaced grass and the borders were redefined with soft layers of green in different textures, shapes, and varieties. "We had one of all sorts of plants and pairs of nothing, so my 'consultant' added two topiary pineapple guavas which annually display exotic pink and red blossoms and small hedges of boxwood and variegated pittosporum," he continued. This helped redefine and harmonize the area. The espaliered pyracantha on the driveway walls opposite the house have been teased into interesting Japonesque shapes, with highly textured holly ferns planted in the narrow bed below. "Polyverdant and very pleasing" is the way Dr. Baldwin now describes it.

A DOUBLE COURTYARD

One of the city's most interesting and private gardens lies within the romantic ruins of an old warehouse hidden behind an eighteenth-century residence in the Historic District. The handsome four-story structure had been rebuilt in the late 1700s, after two of the city's great fires caused significant damage to the early building. It was typical of merchant buildings of the day: the first floor was for business, and the family lived on the top floors of the house. At some point the first floor was a grain and feed store: grain was brought through a narrow alley and stored in the warehouse that was attached to the main house.

Preservation-minded individuals stabilized the walls of the warehouse after it lost its roof and windows. The famous Charleston landscape architect Loutrel Briggs designed and installed a double courtyard for the space in 1941. His basic plan remains today. The plan of this garden and many others,

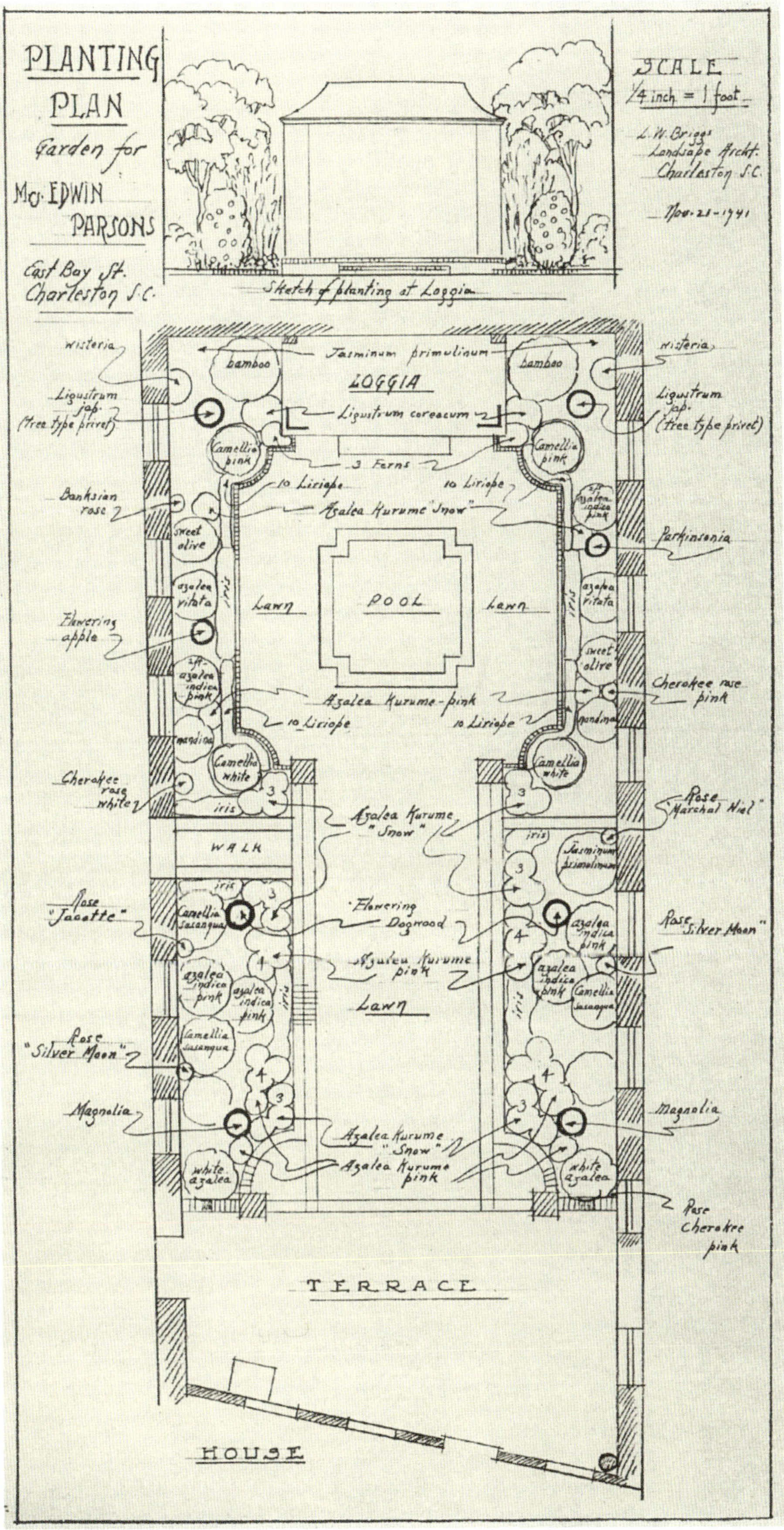

The delicate blue flowers of the flax plant rise above ajuga and chartreuse-colored sedum in a raised planter. *Camellia sasanqua* lines the walls at the old window level and is accentuated by a dwarf boxwood hedge. The coarse leaves of a holly fern add a different texture and also reflect light.

Morning sunlight floods the courtyards in late spring. Fig vine is kept pruned at the top level of the first story of the old warehouse building. The Confederate jasmine surrounding the opening of the folly at the back of the garden has just finished blooming.

revealing Briggs's particular genius, can be found in James Cothran's book *Charleston Gardens and the Landscape Legacy of Loutrel Briggs,* published by the University of South Carolina Press.

When the present owners purchased the property in 2000, they went through more than a year of major renovation, and the Briggs garden, which had already declined, suffered as a construction site. The roof of the little seating folly, as it is called, had collapsed. The pool no longer held water, and all the plants were ruined. Only a pair of crape myrtles and a pair of camellias remained intact. Most of the paving and the open-work brick dividing walls were also undamaged, and, happily, the open brickwork filling the twenty-four windows of the two story walls also remained. Everything, however, was completely covered by rampant fig vines that threatened the entire structure.

The owners consulted a friend, Beverly Rivers, a local gardening expert. She helped them tame the vines and replant the courtyards. John Laurens, another friend and a talented designer, drew up plans for a glassed-in "orangery," for enjoying the view from indoors. The roof of the folly was replaced, the pond was repaired and fitted with a pump to aerate the water, and more trees were added. Now there is a quartet of crape myrtles at each corner of the first courtyard and a mature pair of Washingtonia palms at the far corners of the second and lower courtyard. The palms were too large to carry down the narrow alley that accesses the garden from the street, so they were brought right through the front hall and dining room. Sasanquas once again bloom in the first courtyard, providing late fall and winter color. Ferns and ligularias (farfugium) are planted as accents, and a pair of tea olives adds fragrance when in bloom.

One of the owners inherited her love of gardening from her grandmother, who was a devoted and award-winning gardener. When the great-grandchildren were small, her grandmother flew to Charleston from Alabama with a bushel of hybrid daylilies and helped her granddaughter plant them in the couple's first garden in Charleston.

All of the urns and garden furniture once belonged to this same grandmother, and the owner also inherited her sense of style and design. The courtyards are restrained, but have charming accents and a touch of fancy throughout. The delicate pastel-colored water lilies are a recent addition.

The owners are out in the garden daily. It is a lovely spot for morning coffee, lunch, cocktails, and entertaining. At night, with the lights in the trees and a sweet breeze coming through all the windows, the garden is "absolutely magical and has a European feel to it," they say. They love the privacy and the strong architectural presence of the enclosing walls.

A COURTYARD IN THE FRENCH QUARTER

"We fell in love with Charleston on a visit in March 2010 and moved quickly," the former resident of New England tells me. She and her husband purchased a renovated brick building dating from the 1870s with a second-story wooden addition built around 1900. There was not even an interior staircase until the mid-1980s when the interior was gutted and modernized. It is possible that the now-charming dwelling was once a tobacco shop, but its history is murky.

Entering the light-filled open space, one's eye is immediately drawn through the living room and kitchen to the glass doors that open into a courtyard featuring an unusual wall fountain. Water trickles down through a maze of framed *pavé* oyster shells into a small basin, and a shelf above holds seasonal decorations. The owners thoroughly enjoy creating new displays

An unusual oyster-shell fountain reflects light in the center of the courtyard.

throughout the year. The fountain also lends a modern, whimsical touch to the more formal and traditional seating area. The wooden deck in the center of the courtyard was a solution to the need for access to the crawl space under the house: a wooden hatch door provides entry.

Lit up at night, the courtyard is a cozy place to entertain. A fragrant old tea olive dominates a smaller area to the right of the fountain and softens the view of the walls of neighboring buildings. The tree also gives a bit of privacy and shade to the bench below. On a south-facing wall, a 'Lady Banks' rose is flourishing and is going to be trained onto a pair of antique architectural arches. A small early-spring-blooming tulip magnolia opposite the rose is

Window boxes decorate the exterior and provide extra gardening space.

underplanted with bright blue summer- and fall-blooming plumbago. Pots of topiary lend additional structure as well as color from annuals planted at the base of the clipped ligustrum.

The courtyard serves many functions: it satisfies a love of gardening and creating interesting spaces; it adds room for entertaining; and it is a lovely outdoor place to read and relax. A particularly delightful and amusing bonus, explains one of the owners, is that it "is a place where we often communicate with our immediate neighbors and friends. They just open a window, call down to us, and we chat and make plans."

Peninsula Gardens

THE AUTHOR'S GARDEN

Our downtown garden has undergone several renovations and replantings since we moved here more than thirty years ago, but Hurricane Hugo in 1989, neighboring building projects, and renovations to immediately adjacent properties during the past five years have brought about drastic changes in our small landscape. We began transforming our roughly one-third of an acre from a shaded semiformal garden surrounded by unrestrained clumps of bamboo, wisteria vines, and a small grove of cherry laurel trees into a sunny formal garden with a strong Italian influence.

The current design evolved slowly. Hoping to build another house on the lot that comprised the back of our garden—the less formal area—we removed overgrown hollies and filled in the fifteen-by eight-foot pond in 2010. I missed the song birds, the lotus and lilies, and the fish, but local populations of egrets, neighborhood cats, and raccoons ate the fish and punctured and tore the pond lining, resulting in slow leaks. Debris and lack of maintenance contributed to its becoming a bog. While waiting for our building plans to come to fruition, we allowed morning glories, Virginia creeper, *Tetrapanax* (rice paper plant), bamboo, and crabgrass to take over. This return to nature happened nearly overnight. It only took a summer of neglect for the back garden to look absolutely abandoned. I tried growing a few vegetables and some herbs, but the area remained a weedy mess. We had carpenters install a substantial lattice-work fence with a gate, separating it from the formal part of the garden that we still maintained. Then, in the summer of 2011 the enormous *Magnolia grandiflora* that dominated our garden became a threat. It had lifted and pushed out the brick wall enclosing and protecting us all along our northern property line, which is on a busy street. The tree's aggressive root system had long since been problematic in such a small space, and the buckets of leaves that dropped daily throughout the year were messy and time-consuming to rake and pick out of the flowerbeds and lawn. We had to obtain permission from the city for its removal: it now measured as a "grand tree." We were astonished by the light and the space that opened up with its demise.

The next exciting event occurred a month later in September. The unoccupied house on the western lot line, which we faced as we entered the garden from the house and the drive, was sold and a complete renovation began. We gave permission for temporary removal of a portion of the high wooden fence separating our properties along the southwestern border,

FACING A sandstone carriage block found on the property supports a statue of Eros at the terminus of the main garden. The small tree is *Cercis canadensis* 'Hearts of Gold'.

The back lot in 2012

as well as permission to cut down our tall bamboo screen that hid the dilapidated house. We had workmen in our garden for five months and were delighted at last to see the new siding, new roof, and rebuilt arched brick chimneys on the late antebellum structure that forms our western boundary.

Our plan to build a small house on the lot did not work out, and we decided to reclaim and embrace the garden in its entirety. We removed most of the lattice-work dividing fence. Then we hired a crew to dig out bamboo, fell cherry laurels, and grind stumps. Our garden opened up to us, sunlit and promising.

Presented with a relatively bare canvas, my artistic husband went to work. He drew out numerous designs on graph paper, mapped out potential walks and patios with pieces of hose and brick, and discussed variations with his close friend E. G. Johnson III, whose garden design work is shown elsewhere in this book.

There was a surprising amount of old stones and bricks lying around the property. We soon discovered even more as we shoveled deep holes for planting, grubbed out vines, and chopped out roots and stumps with hatchet, axe, and saw. Someone had tossed out lovely pieces of marble fireplace surrounds that remained intact, buried behind the bamboo. Our house was built by 1773, and we suspect that these pieces were original to the building and discarded when coal grates were placed in some of the fireplaces. We have unearthed hundreds of bits of china, a George II coin, buttons, beads, bottles, animal bones, and even the top set of some false teeth. Chunks of Bermuda stone, a millstone, hundreds of cobblestones and bricks, gray slabs full of fossils, and a few flagstones and Belgian blocks were gathered into

Part of the same area shown above, one year later, featuring a trompe l'oeil arch inspired by tessellated tiles from a seventeenth-century church in Lisbon

piles for later use. Several old carriage blocks and limestone blocks were to become benches and plinths. Robert Johnson, a skilled brick mason, started work on edgings and layout as the design took shape, adding patios and paths.

Repetition is one of our garden's most effective design elements. Combining repetition with symmetry, color, texture, and shape, my husband decided on a dramatic planting of an ellipse of sixteen Italian cypresses embracing the end of the longest east-west axis, the view one glimpses when entering the front hall of the house. A small cistern and statue with a fountain in front of a lattice-work arch was already in place at this terminus of the garden, as were the two rectangular parterres with a circular raised bed in the center. The property is L-shaped, so he wanted an equally dramatic element for the shorter north-south axis.

Years before, he had designed and ordered a quartet of metal structures, tuteurs in the shape of obelisks, to contain podocarpus shrubs. More were ordered, and now seven of them, filled with this slow-growing evergreen bush nicknamed Southern yew, surround a circular lawn at the end of a wide flagstone path leading off at a right angle to the main garden. A millstone punctuates the center of the circle. An eighth tuteur containing an unusual blue-green podocarpus cultivar, set in the central parterre, repeats the pyramidal plantings throughout. Balanced plantings of shrubs (*Loropetalum,*

A view of the garden from a neighbor's deck in late May shows the circular lawn surrounded by newly planted shrubs and tuteurs containing podocarpus.

variegated euonymus, plumbago, and camellia) and small trees (*Cercis*, hollies, crape myrtles, figs, and *Magnolia × soulangiana*) add rhythm and color in the background. Dwarf boxwood hedges punctuated by boxwood balls outline the beds. The bamboo is growing back slowly, and we are carefully keeping it well pruned. We need it to provide a tall, soft screen against the bare facade of the neighbors' wooden siding.

My husband, Price, took on the burden of most of the planting, including the new trees; hundreds of containers all told. Frequent trips to the nurseries resulted in the discovery of new varieties of trees and shrubs that are exciting additions. One of our favorites is *Cercis canadensis* 'Hearts of Gold', a redbud tree with chartreuse heart-shaped leaves. Price made dozens of additional trips for soil amendments: mushroom compost, peat moss, and cow manure. The old dirt was just exhausted. Azaleas, camellias, and gardenias prefer acidic soil, and the mortar from the old brick walls slowly leaches lime into the soil year after year, rendering it just the opposite: alkaline. During a period when coal fires were burned in the house, the fireplace ashes were thrown out into the yard. I diligently dispose of even the smallest bits constantly found in the dirt, as coal is poisonous to plants.

We had purchased a blue and white mural of tiles (*azulejos*) while traveling in Portugal in 2002 and had always hoped to use it to good effect.

A view of one of three arches covered with 'Climbing Pinkie' roses. Three of the eight tondi are in the background. Larkspur and Confederate jasmine are coming into full bloom.

Price cut an arch into the thick fig vine covering one of our long stucco walls, painted the surface a deep terra-cotta, and designed a tabernacle of brick and stone to contain the tiles. Inspired by both books and travel, he continued the arches at intervals, painted more tabernacles and tiles in trompe l'oeil, and is adding tondi with della Robbia designs in them.

To emphasize the painted arches in the wall, metal arbors planted with 'Climbing Pinkie' roses and gloriosa lilies were placed in front of them. These are warm sunny spots in the winter and cooler fragrant shady spots in the late summer afternoons, so we added benches just wide enough to seat two. We removed a section of azaleas and oak leaf hydrangeas and added more

Poppies, old roses, larkspur, geraniums, and the berries of the nandina shrub mix with the new bright leaves of mint, boxwood, and the fig tree in spring.

Clerodendrum indicum, commonly known as Turk's Turban, is spectacular in the fall garden.

room for sitting: a brick patio in the shade beneath the line of crape myrtles on our southern border. Against this wall a colorful trio of trompe l'oeil–tiled arches feature lions' heads spouting water into simple basins.

We have placed seating all around the garden and especially enjoy our flagstone patio furnished with a marble-topped table and four lyre-backed chairs. It is delightful to enjoy the sweet sea breezes and have dinner outside with friends while watching the moon come up between church steeples across the street. The center of this patio has my husband's archeological ecclesiastical design featuring a cross made of the marble we found buried at the edge of the property. White Bermuda stone, orchard stone, flagstone, and bits of china and glass found in the garden complete the pattern. An old metal aquarium stand just the right size and sturdy enough to hold an extra piece of marble that was on hand works well as a small serving table.

When we moved here three decades ago, there was very little structure to the old yard, and it was chock-full of plants with minds of their own. We have bullied the remaining bamboo into submission and finally gotten rid of the last of numerous cherry laurel trees. George Schenck, in his book on shade gardens, said that "planting a cherry laurel is an act of aggression against one's neighbor." We have been plagued not only by the hundreds of thousands of its seedlings that come up everywhere and the tree's noxious pollen, but also by the flocks of cedar waxwings who love to feed on the ripe berries and then cover our non-garaged cars with their gluelike droppings. I am still fighting the rice-paper plant (*Tetrapanax papyriferus*) we unwittingly imported, the ivy that covers our south walls but also runs furiously through the shade beds, the tiny red-stemmed spurge that never goes away, and the Virginia creeper and wisteria that consistently and aggressively propagate by runner and by seeds the birds drop. I once snitched some cashmere bouquet (*Clerodendrum bungei*) from a graveyard and was punished for my thievery for years afterward. The flower head is fragrant, but the leaves have a foul odor and the plant is difficult to control. A website selling it suggests keeping it pot-bound. The same advice applies strongly to the alstroemeria species lily, as we found out the hard way. I have been digging it out of the shrubs for twenty years. Crinum lilies are fascinating old plants but can also get out of hand in a small garden. Trying suspected "thugs" in pots before setting them out into the flower beds is now policy.

Our new garden scheme features symmetry and repetition of small trees and shrubbery that are performance-reliable, including *Loropetalum rubrum,* hollies, *Magnolia* × *soulangiana,* boxwoods, variegated euonymus, and hardy roses. Within this framework experimentation with new and unusual, heirloom or out-of-fashion plant material does not ruin the overall effect and can have interesting results rather than a jumbled look.

Hydrangeas, camellias, large holly ferns *(Cyrtomium falcatum),* gold dust shrub (*Aucuba*), cast-iron plant (*Aspidistra elatior*), and azaleas work well in the shady areas, as do many varieties of common ferns. These are relatively low-maintenance plants that provide both color and texture. Scale and other pests require spraying or careful husbandry but can be controlled. Ivy can get out of hand quickly; I like the slower-growing jasmine, ajuga, *Ardisia japonica,* and strawberry begonias (*Saxifraga stolonifera*) for shade ground covers and the easily controlled and colorful potato vine or the trailing lantana for hot sunny spots. Shade-tolerant gardenias and ginger lilies are valued for their heady fragrance, new types of cannas for their verticality and bright colors. Out of sentiment, we have left a few crocosmia bulbs and Indian shot cannas from the original garden we found when we moved here.

I love planting annuals and sowing seeds. Lettuces and other edible greens are fun to harvest in early spring and are soft and pretty. Arugula and warm-weather spinach also grow well in our climate. Accent plants are easy to change from year to year and provide instant color and gaiety. One year I might plant pots with pansies for spring, then another time try hyacinths and daffodils or whatever strikes my fancy at the nursery. I adore geraniums, especially in all the deep shades, and am always willing to try something different. There is a lot of color from the reseeding annuals such as larkspur, marigolds, and poppies, and they sprout in unexpected places. Spring bulbs

OVERLEAF A view of the house and the Lutheran and Unitarian church steeples in the late fall

are not reliable repeat performers for us because of the squirrels and my lack of patience to wait for the leaves to turn completely brown before removing them. If the dying leaves are removed too early, the bulbs do not get adequate food for next year's bloom. Caladium bulbs are cool and crisp in a summer garden and light up shady areas, but they often need to be dug in the fall or replaced. Impatiens is a reliable, stellar performer. Lilies of the Nile (*Agapanthus*) and crinum lilies are good choices for summer and come in dwarf varieties. There are many ways to use succulents.

Mulch, to my surprise, can be controversial. I attended a lecture by an Englishwoman who declared that "Americans just love their mulch; we English tend to plant ground covers and other plants instead of using it." Well, I was thrilled when two dump trucks full of rich dark mulch arrived in June 2012 and a pair of men working hoses sprayed the lovely dark shredded bark under every bush and into every weed-laden nook and cranny. Mulch keeps the plant roots cool, cuts down on disease, prevents many types of weeds from germinating, softens the formerly dirt paths in some areas, and makes the greens and other colors sing louder. I do like ground covers, too, and will work to establish nonaggressive ones, but this is the South, and, as a cousin once remarked, "You have to beat the foliage back with a broomstick." Mulch offers a degree of control.

Our lawn was damaged in the aftermath of Hurricane Hugo in 1989. It never recovered from compaction after workmen spent eight days taking out trees. The twelve-foot diameter hole that resulted when a sixty-foot water oak was uprooted was filled in but left the ground uneven. All sorts of weeds blew in and established themselves. The final blow was a malfunction in the watering system a couple of years ago. We under- then overwatered, and the lawn was eaten up by weeds, fungus, and chinch bugs. We have just installed a new zoysia lawn. This is a major departure from the traditional St. Augustine grass, and I think it adds to the European atmosphere. The removal and cutting back of overgrown and out-of-scale shrubs and trees has let in enough additional light to allow hope that the lawn will thrive. We have to high-prune the crape myrtles growing at intervals along the walls and flatten their silhouettes every two or three years.

I suspect that the current design will be tweaked and retweaked as there are still areas needing paths, focal points, and pretty plants. Our neighbor to the south, a school, has been a pleasure to work with on the colors of the facades seen from our garden, allowing us to choose rosy browns, terra-cottas, and greens. We will plant small flowering trees against these favorable backgrounds and perhaps some noninvasive vines to soften them. A twenty-year-old ginkgo tree, purchased as a male, suddenly started bearing great crops of foul-smelling fruit and had to be removed.

We will always look forward to weeding, pruning, clipping, deadheading, harvesting, and planting new combinations, then delighting in the results at the end of the day. It is a never-ending joy we share with our family, friends, neighbors, and visitors. I am so deeply grateful for a garden and for those who appreciate our efforts.

THE GARDEN OF THE JAMES BROWN HOUSE (CA. 1768)

The typical Charleston single-house plan offers an interesting challenge to modern gardeners. One scholar's interpretation is that "the single house was a creative response to the increasing scarcity of space in the city and was designed to mitigate the unpleasantness of hot, humid summers. With its narrow side directly on the street, the rectangular house with two rooms in each story grew tall to raise the main entertaining room to the level of the prevailing breeze which passed through a side piazza. As a free-standing house communicating more with a side garden than with the street, the single house offered a masterful but still vernacular solution to the residential problems of achieving comfort, privacy, and propriety."

Often built on narrow adjacent lots, these one-room-wide houses frequently had extensions and separate dependency buildings with their own entrances. A carriageway was incorporated into the original designs of the grander houses. Today, parking automobiles presents a considerable problem for most owners and garden designers, especially in the Historic District where modern garages are not common. The porches, or piazzas, usually faced south or west, thus overlooking a garden with a northern, shady exposure opposite or with the morning eastern light frequently blocked in part by the house itself. The wider the property, the less extreme is the lack of light.

Dr. and Mrs. Leigh Thompson returned home to Charleston in the 1990s after a long interval and purchased a single house downtown. It had an ample lot and enough space between the main house and the original kitchen building for construction of a "hyphen" multistory addition that included a garage on the ground floor. Work on the garden began in 1995 after the construction was finished. More improvements were completed much later.

As an ardent fan of puzzles, Dr. Thompson decided that the garden's main feature would be a maze surrounding a fountain to be prominently displayed in the front of the property and visible from the sidewalk through the wrought-iron fence. The maze is constructed of brick and pebbles with boxwood accents. It is perfectly symmetrical and uses historical and religious design elements. Mrs. Thompson explains: "In China the central circle represents heaven and the outer square represents earth. To the Japanese the lines radiating from the center represent the rays of the rising sun. The cross is that of the French Protestant Huguenots, who used it as their symbol while fleeing persecution at home and seeking freedom, many in Charleston. The points of the cross represent the eight beatitudes of the Sermon on the Mount."

The fun begins with the solutions to the maze, which Dr. Thompson worked out on the computer. There are only two correct solutions and more than 313 billion incorrect ones. In both correct solutions one has to touch all vertices of the square and all points of the cross. There are eight four-choice points and fourteen three-choice points, and each walk is eighty-five feet long. According to its creator, if you were to walk all alternative paths both ways, including all twenty-two branch points, you would have a brisk healthy walk of ten billion miles.

The podocarpus shrubs along the drive are clipped into rectangular prisms, echoing the shape of the bricks in the maze and around the fountain.

The Thompsons had Robert Stockton, a well-known local historian, research a complete history of the property, but there was no record at all of the colonial garden. A few of the plants and crape myrtles dated from the 1940s and were retained, as were the boxwoods, which had been propagated from George Washington's own Mount Vernon specimens.

The maze, viewed from the second-story piazza.

Botany Bay Landscaping was hired to plant and maintain the garden and an abundant sidewalk display. "We wanted the driveway to look like a garden path and the palmettos and roses in front are my 'No Parking' signs," says Mrs. Thompson with a smile; "the trees prevent service trucks and other vehicles from pulling onto the low sidewalk." As shown on the garden plan pictured below, the maze is partially repeated in the parking turnaround, against the wall of the house next door to the south. The lawn, which is Charleston grass (St. Augustine), is repeated in front of the guest house. A quartet of flowering cherry trees provides shade and often a spectacular display in spring.

Plenty of seating is provided by a low knee wall along the drive, granite and metal work benches throughout, and comfortable chairs and chaise lounges on the piazzas.

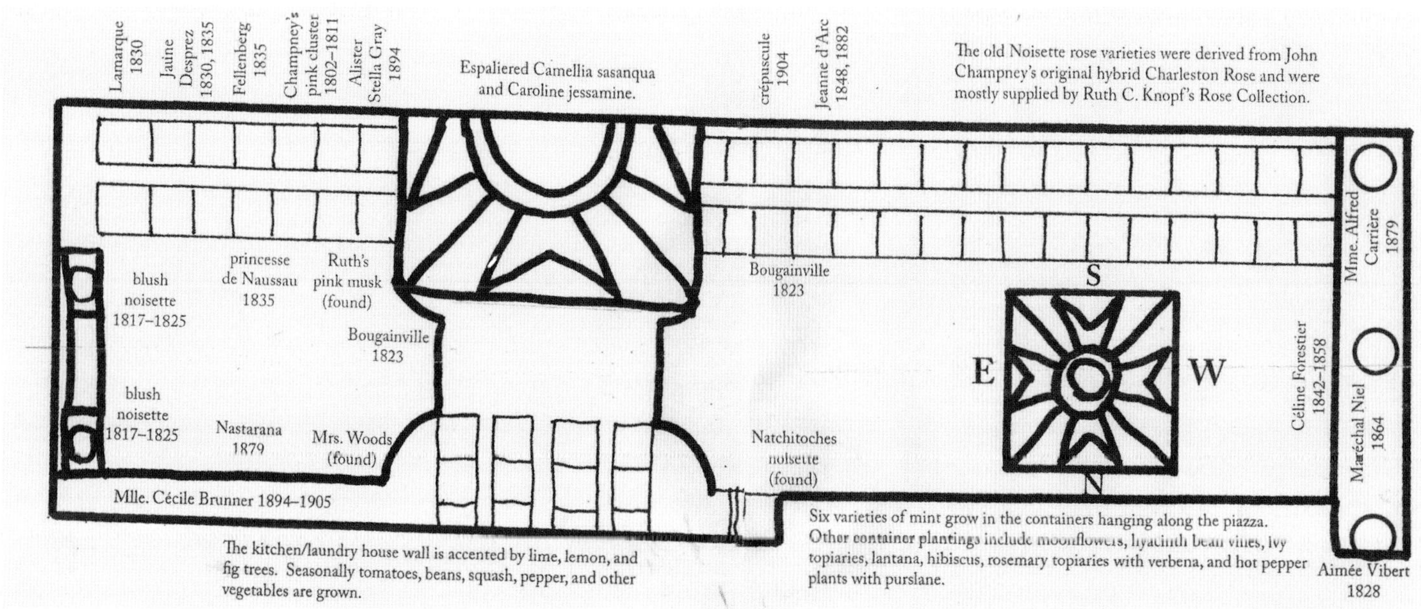

Plan of the garden. Courtesy of the owner.

A notable feature of the garden is the collection of Noisette roses, the first class of roses hybridized in America, planted as shown in the plan above. A 'Rêve d'Or' rose, not shown above, is also part of the collection and is entwined around a fourth palmetto to the north of the 'Aimée Vibert.'

History of Roses: Noisette Roses

Noisettes, like several other classes of Old Garden Roses, came about by chance.

The Noisette roses can be traced back to the time when a rice farmer in Charleston, South Carolina, named John Champney received 'Old Blush' (also known as 'Parsons' Pink China', a China rose that had been growing in China and Asia for more than a thousand years), as a gift from his neighbor, Philippe Noisette.

Philippe Noisette came from a family of distinguished horticulturists in France. He arrived in Charleston, South Carolina, from France, via Haiti, around 1800. Philippe became the superintendent of the South Carolina Medical Society's Botanical Garden. A large tract of land was purchased on the outskirts of the city where there was room for gardens and a nursery. This became known as the Noisette farm.

John Champney crossed 'Old Blush' with 'Rosa moschata', a 1540 species rose from the Himalayas. This resulted in 'Champneys' Pink Cluster' (before 1810), a major contribution from an American grower to the rose family. John Champney then gave Philippe seedlings of 'Champneys' Pink Cluster' in return for Philippe's having given John 'Old Blush'. Philippe sowed the seeds of 'Champneys' Pink Cluster' and produced 'Blush Noisette', which he sent to his brother Louis (Philippe had fifteen siblings . . .) in France in 1814.

This started a new craze to breed a group of roses known as the Noisettes. Thomas Rivers wrote about 'Blush Noisette' or 'Rosier Noisette' in *The Rose Amateur's Guide* in 1877. "Perhaps no new rose was ever so much admired as this. When first introduced its habit was so peculiar, and so unlike any other known variety, that the Parisian amateurs were quite enraptured with it." [Pierre-Joseph] Redouté painted 'Blush Noisette' in 1821 under the name Rosa noisettiana. The rose was also classified and described by the botanist Claude-Antoine Thory to accompany the Redouté.

The early Noisettes combined the broad, shrubby habit, and scented large clusters of the Musk Roses with the pink coloring, larger flowers and continuous blooming pattern of the Chinas. 'Blush Noisette' is blush colored, but other varieties come in a spectrum of colors ranging from pure white to crimson. Around 1825, French rose breeders tried to hybridize yellow Noisettes by crossing 'Blush Noisette' with 'Parks' Yellow Tea-Scented China'. This produced many great beauties. When the early Noisettes (Musk x China) were crossed with Teas, they produced the Tea-Noisettes.

A 'Celine Forestier' rose in bloom on the front fence. This rose, with its spicy scent, was bred by V. Trouillard in 1842 and can grow canes up to fifteen feet long. Photograph by Mrs. Leigh Thompson

[Written by Jerry Haynes, this was part of his award-winning series of articles on the history of roses written for the American Rose Society's website (courtesy of the American Rose Society)]

Ethelyn Emery Keays wrote that the class of Tea-Noisettes received larger blooms of greater substance and a sweeter fragrance: "Tea-Noisettes are greatly prized as some of the most beautiful roses you will ever find in warmer climates that do not have frost or chill."

According to Mrs. Thompson, the garden is very personal—idiosyncratic, in fact. The primary focus is on the Noisette roses, but she is also interested in growing edibles among the flowers and in propagating plants.

View of the house facing west

A pair of potted avocado trees that are protected if there is a threat of frost stands on either side of the steps from the piazza into the garden. There are also citrus trees in pots, including lemon; kaffir, key, and Persian limes; kumquat; and the calamondin orange. This orange can tolerate cold to twenty degrees Fahrenheit, making it hardier than any other true citrus—only the trifoliate orange and the kumquat are more tolerant to low temperatures.

A fig and a loquat tree also provide fruit, and vegetable plantings are scattered about, mostly in pots. A large container with lettuces ("the lettuce bowl") is available outside the kitchen door in the winter.

Cilantro, lemongrass, rosemary, and parsley are favorite herbs, along with mint plants in their hanging planters along the lower piazza. "I like to offer my guests their libation of choice with their mint of choice," says Mrs. Thompson.

THE GARDEN OF THE ISAAC MOTTE DART HOUSE

In 1995 Dr. Eugene G. Johnson and his wife, Elizabeth, purchased a significant property from Historic Charleston Foundation. Consisting of a fine early-nineteenth-century mansion, a carriage house with gothic architectural elements, and a parking lot for the former school on the property, it sat on nearly half an acre. It took several years to renovate and restore the houses and several more for Dr. Johnson's vision of a garden to grow to completion.

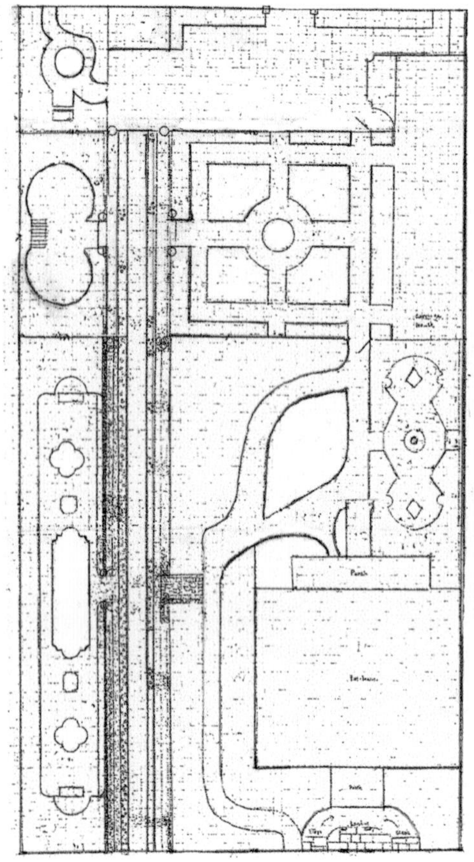

The garden plan, drawn by Eugene G. Johnson

The design was not only his own; he and his family did most of the work as well: removing the old asphalt, spreading truckloads of topsoil, and adding more truckloads of soil amendments, including compost recycled at the city landfill. Today six separate gardens flank a central drive that leads to a generous parking area hidden behind one of the two scalloped picket fences built to embrace a parterre garden in front of the carriage house. Dr. Johnson sketched out a different pattern for each garden room and planted hundreds of boxwoods, azaleas, camellias, sasanquas, loropetalums, podocarpus, pittosporums, hydrangeas, and other flowering shrubs and vines. There were only two trees on the entire lot: a palmetto and a venerable, enormous Darlington oak that provided high shade. Strips of St. Augustine lawn, rows of crape myrtles, and a hedge of hollies and Italian cypresses were planted to further define boundaries, both within and at the edges of the property. Paths of gray slag, wide enough for two to stroll side by side, were edged with old brick and laid out in both geometric and meandering patterns.

An herb garden with lemon and lime trees in wooden containers and tuteurs for climbing plants was also integrated into the design and situated in traditional fashion near the kitchen of the house. Like the rest of the garden, this is a formal area with a strong pattern. Accent plants were added slowly and with consideration for color and effect. Some of the herbs were constantly plagued with slugs and insects, but the solution turned out to be funfilled. A garden cart, formerly used by the grandchildren, is now filled with pots of parsley, basil, and other plants used for cooking and is pulled around the garden to sunny or irrigated areas. More interesting changes took place in the garden as the Johnsons discovered new plants and their travels inspired them with fresh ideas. The recent addition of a stunning piece of modern sculpture lends a brilliant focal point for another of the smaller garden rooms that has a large table and plenty of seating for entertaining al fresco.

The Johnsons also tried plants that did *not* work well in the confines of a city garden. Laughing at himself not only for planting bamboo and wisteria but also for fertilizing them, Dr. Johnson remembers that it took him years

The driveway entrance to the property. Dr. Johnson also designed the gothic-style garden folly at the end of the drive. Crape myrtles shade a border of azaleas and sasanquas on the right.

to get rid of the lovely, but aggressive, grass and vine. The bamboo ran underground and popped up halfway across the lot in "no time." "Wherever I pushed my shovel into the ground to plant something, I'd hit another knotty rhizome and have to dig it out completely." Other not-so-successful plants were ruthlessly destroyed or given away; the garden is kept extremely neat and clean, adding to its spacious and small estatelike feel.

In 2005, ten years after starting his garden from scratch, Dr. Johnson became a finalist in Good Morning America's contest for the year's best amateur garden designer. Then he took a course from landscape architect Mary Palmer Dargan and became certified in landscape design. His first contract

A glimpse of the formal garden along the driveway through the branches of one of the crape myrtles planted by the back porch

was an enormous undertaking and launched his new career after his retirement from medical practice.

The garden has matured beautifully and become even more appealing. Dr. Johnson designed a brick garden building with pointed arches in the gothic style that now sits at the north end of the cobbled drive that dissects the entire lot. Darlington oaks have an average life expectancy of about 150 to 175 years; the age of their oak was estimated at more than 200 years, and it died a natural death. Its necessary removal was a sad chapter in the property's history. But the unfiltered light has allowed many other plants and trees

Dappled light makes patterns on the lawn of the herb garden and the brick wall of the dependency building.

to prosper. The red maple is no longer a sapling and the crape myrtles are looking statuesque. A rose and lily bed in a paisley shape is thriving.

Maintenance is the biggest challenge. When asked what he wished for most for his garden now, Dr. Johnson replied, "a staff of six." His vision for the future is stasis; keeping the plant material in scale and healthy. Frustrated with lawn problems, he recently had zoysia grass put in place of the St. Augustine. He still does almost all of the pruning, clipping, and weeding, but he does get help trimming the high hedge of East Palatka hollies that alternate between the enormous Italian cypresses and form the garden's western border. He occasionally hires help for other large tasks. Spraying for leaf scale and fungal diseases is done professionally. The work, he notes, can

Formal parterres of boxwood were planted in front of the carriage house.

Seen from the house, the statuary garden is just visible through summer foliage.

be overwhelming, but he now takes his time. "I used to be determined to get the garden pulled together in a day or two, but now I take a section at time, ignoring the weeds elsewhere as I focus on the task at hand. Eventually it all comes together."

THE GARDEN OF THE ALBERT DETMAR HOUSE (CA. 1770)

Behind one of Charleston's pre-Revolutionary masonry single houses is a garden that has played a major role in the lives of its owners for the past forty years. Best known to Charlestonians as one of Loutrel Briggs's finest designs for small spaces, the garden was landscaped in the 1960s. An interesting exchange had taken place: the neighbors to the south gave a narrow northern strip of land along the property line in trade for a western rectangle that extended behind the Detmar house. This allowed for off-street parking, which was becoming a necessity, and the present garden boundaries took shape.

Briggs's design played on circles within circles. The driveway led into a rectangle embraced by the house, then up a level to a semi-enclosed area with a statue in a round and shallow central pool. Up one more step to the third level, a horseshoe-shaped bed planted with boxwoods surrounded a columnar sundial. There was a storage space to the right at the very back and a greenhouse with substantial glass and wood doors. The walls, paving,

The fish pond adds sound, motion, and color to the courtyard.

fountains, steps, and brick borders comprised nearly 80 percent of the plan on paper, with flagstone, slate, and brick used for most of the hardscape. A pierced brick wall at the far end of the garden allowed for air circulation and added another design element. Various shrubs and small trees were carefully chosen to fill out the borders. During the next thirty years, the garden matured beautifully and was considered a showpiece, as it was well tended and gaily planted out with colorful annuals.

Briggs's hardscape remained intact, but in the first decade of this century subsequent owners retained another well-known local landscape architect,

Sheila Wertimer, who deleted most of the driveway and added a low rectilinear goldfish pool with water spouts and brick edges wide enough for seating. The greenhouse was removed and replaced with a white wooden pergola covered in roses and clematis. The circular fountain was filled with bog plants, the boxwoods were taken out, and garden ornaments were rearranged and replaced. The emphasis was on lush, tropical-looking plant material, and the whole garden took on a much softer, less formal look.

When the present owners moved in, they wanted to make the garden more formal again and began restoring it with many of the same plants used by Loutrel Briggs. They were even able to procure a copy of the Pan statue in the fountain used in the 1969 design. Boxwoods were replanted to emphasize the horseshoe shape at the end of the garden. There have been interesting additions and tweaks. A mature, dying tree had to be removed, and the owners paved the small area that used to be beneath the tree with a clever diamond pattern of slate and small cobblestones. Brightly striped cushions on garden furniture are welcoming accents.

More touches include a taste for unusual plants, as well as an eye for using many different textures. There is a weeping camellia in a large pot, a pair of white *Pieris japonica* ('Temple Bells') flank the step up to the middle level; hellebores bloom along the goldfish pond; and a weeping *Ilex vomitoria* shades part of the southern border. A seldom seen Nun's Orchid (*Phaius grandifolius*) has survived for several seasons, although the owners thought it was an annual. Lively and personal, the garden is often used and much enjoyed.

Morning glories cascade over the entrance gate to the garden.

AN ARTISTIC GARDEN

The multiple talents and ideas of a pair of artists (who are also a poet and a surgeon) and an award-winning landscape architect were combined in a very small space to create a garden with a whimsical, romantic, and exotic atmosphere.

Intrigued by gardens they had visited abroad, the owners wanted to transform their roughly two-thousand-square-foot yard into something unusual and different from the typical Charleston garden; they did, however, want it to reflect their tastes and also to fit in with a Charleston lifestyle. They wanted a place for their children to congregate with friends, a place for entertaining, and a place for quiet contemplation and pleasure.

In 1992 they had built a two-story addition onto their eighteenth-century downtown residence, further reducing the size of the yard. But the addition, which mimicked a carriage house, was intimately integrated with the outside: it had ten glassed-in arches looking out from a generous family room and kitchen.

Sallie Drury Iselin, a landscape designer and friend of the owners, helped with some of the first plantings in what then amounted to a blank slate. Italian cypresses planted between the arches softened the walls of the new addition, while palmettos and palms helped define the perimeters of the L-shaped grassy plot that remained.

But it was a trip to Spain in 2001 and the book *Gardens of Delight: The Great Islamic Gardens*, by Christa Von Hantlemann, that inspired them to enlist the talents of a local landscape architect, Sheila Wertimer, to create a garden of the senses. The spiritual nature of the gardens of the Moors was highly appealing to the owners, and they felt that Charleston had some similar elements: a hot climate, enclosure, and privacy in many of its peninsula gardens.

The entrance court includes palms, banana trees, and papyrus plants.

Parking spaces are of great importance to city residents and can be difficult to integrate into an overall garden design. On this property an allowance was made to the side of the house where several cars could be parked. Wide gates fronting the street were designed by the owner, who also designed a smaller gate within a stucco wall leading to the garden from the parking area. Decorative paving materials form patterns that are repeated in the paving just within the gates. To the side is a small seating area installed by Lance Leader that features a fountain and benches, lending a formal touch to the entrance with its bright blue front door.

The garden is distinctive. As you enter, your eye is pulled along a line of black and white inlaid tiles suggesting a channel, or rill, of water leading to an arched loggia with stone columns. The bluestone path is lined on either side with terra-cotta pots of fruit-bearing citrus trees underplanted with colorful annuals. The loggia, furnished with ceiling fans, cushioned chairs, and a settee, is cool and inviting. Immediately in front of its dais, there is a pair of sunken pools, and a third pool wraps around the side of the loggia in the deep shade. The original design included a fourth pool just inside the entry gate centered on the rill, but because it was necessary to step carefully around it to access the path, it was eventually paved over.

The loggia is bathed in cooling shade.

A narrow rectangular patch of lawn is a transition from the exotic garden to the house and is separated from the rill by a low traditional boxwood hedge. In addition to the loggia for entertaining and dining alfresco, there are an iron table and chairs tucked under a magnolia and an open arched area just off of the kitchen. Statuary of all sorts is centered on axes, some pieces are paired like sentinels along paths, and others are scattered throughout the plants growing beneath the palms and the bamboo.

The five senses played a part in the choice of plant material. The hairy, rough bark and fronds of a variety of palms are visually and physically tactile, and there is also the delight of the velvety, colorful blossoms of bright

A view of the walkway from the loggia

blue morning glories and red geraniums set in a jungle of bamboo, palms, elephant ears, and cycads. The aural sense is satisfied not only by birdsong breaking the early morning silence but also by the cacophony of frogs and toads at dusk or the barking of the dogs enjoying a squirrel chase. And there is the perfume of jasmine and gardenias and of fragrant lemons and limes that are harvested along with the figs and the bananas.

At night the loggia glows with candlelight, and the frogs sing and the sea breeze comes in off the harbor. In this sheltered microclimate, the owners now have the pleasure of their garden of earthly delights all year long.

A lion statue guards the lemon trees.

THE GARDEN OF THE GAILLARD-BENNETT HOUSE

The Gaillard-Bennett House sits on one and one-half acres, making it one of the largest residential properties on the peninsula. The imposing late Federal house was built in 1800, but the Regency portico and steps were added about twenty years later. The house was never entirely neglected, but by the early twenty-first century, the significant outbuildings had fallen into disrepair, a portion of the property had been subdivided, and the garden had dwindled down to lawn with a few trees and shrubs.

In 2004 Steven and Dr. Mary Caroline Stewart, who are both dedicated preservationists, took on the daunting task of restoring the entire property. They had visited Charleston in previous years and had fallen in love with the city. Their extraordinary efforts have won awards. Not only did they restore the main house down to the smallest detail, but they also restored the kitchen house and the stable and carriage house. The charming tack house, which had been destroyed or had fallen down from neglect, was rebuilt. Old photographs and the tack-house foundation gave enough information for an accurate reconstruction. Walls surrounding the urban estate were repaired and constructed, completely enclosing the compound.

A stroke of luck resulted in the reacquisition of a portion of the garden on the southeast side of the property that had been sold many years ago. This lot, squeezed between the Gaillard-Bennett House and the Dart mansion next door and surrounded by a chain-link fence, had a one-story brick

One of the formal gardens is viewed from the eastern balcony, with the roof of the pool house just visible to the left. The lawn in the background is part of the lot that had been subdivided from the property and was reacquired by the current owners. Blue lilies of the Nile fill boxwood parterres around the water-jet fountain.

veneer building on it that the Stewarts demolished to reclaim the area as a garden.

The garden was a blank slate. Sheila Wertimer, a talented and well-known landscape architect who had years of experience working with the City of Charleston on large projects such as Hampton Park, was asked to plan the garden.

The Stewarts had visited gardens of friends and many gardens on the annual tours that take place in the spring and fall to benefit the Preservation Society and Historic Charleston Foundation. Dr. Mary Caroline Stewart took notes and began collecting books on Charleston and southern gardens,

The reconstructed tack house, stable, and kitchen building are set off by thick lawn beneath four crape myrtles. Simple plantings of yew, boxwood, and shade-loving ground covers allow the architecture to dominate.

including ones on native southern plants. She chose her favorite plants and began a master list. She and her husband agreed that they wanted a series of garden rooms featuring fountains and seating areas. They wanted the rooms immediately surrounding the house to reflect its formality and the rooms toward the back of the property to be less formal. It was important to be able to enjoy the garden and entertain in it. The solution was to build a saltwater pool at the back of the property and an elegant but comfortable and modern pool house with an outdoor kitchen, grill, and amenities. The domed pool house is elevated and private and has several seating areas. It overlooks nearly all of the garden with the handsome house in the background.

The west garden runs the length of the house. Boxwood parterres have citrus trees underplanted with society garlic.

Shown above is one of many fountains throughout the garden. This one is in a small courtyard surrounded by fragrant gardenias.

There was a great deal of heavy equipment and construction traffic on the property for several years, so the garden was installed in stages. Several magnolias and hollies needed to be moved with a tree spade, but not much else was in the way of the plans.

The layout is rectilinear, with many focal points on the axes. There are more than a half dozen fountains, large and small. The music of the water tempers the sound of traffic on the busy streets to the south and west, and the birds delight in the sprays and drinking pools. Most of the formal garden can be viewed and accessed from the lovely balconies on either side of the house.

An allée of cherry trees blossoms in the spring, just before the rose bed blooms and the agapanthus lilies put on a spectacular show. The garden is large enough to accommodate masses of crinum lilies, a rose garden, a soft green lawn, and a cutting garden with a picket fence and arbor. Utility areas and equipment are all hidden behind doors. There is even an outside area for the family dogs, fenced in with decorative cast iron.

Each room in the garden is different. To the west of the house, there is a quartet of Meyer lemon trees underplanted with the reliable and care-free

A wall fountain by the northeast terrace leading to the pool house is nearly hidden by agapanthus lilies in full bloom.

society garlic. Low boxwood hedges surround the citrus, and a small fountain marks the center. A formal eastern courtyard has a central raised fountain and pool surrounded by four boxwood parterres punctuated with a single round boxwood in the center of each. Lilies fill the beds. Six Italian cypresses form an elliptical background for the seating area overlooking the spraying jets of the pool.

The area in front of the swimming pool has plants that flower in peach to orange shades. Dr. Stewart enjoys propagating plants and has started several varieties of hydrangeas from leaf cuttings. These shrubs thrive in the shady northern part of the garden. She is a practicing veterinarian and had wanted to have several laying hens tucked away on the property, but her husband talked her out of it. Visitors are amused by the substitute: small and colorful statues of chickens pecking away in one of the flowerbeds. All different sorts and sizes of ceramic, stone, and plaster frogs are hidden in the beds as well—a whimsical touch. Real hens might not have lasted long, given that Mr. Stewart rescued a female red-tailed hawk caught in the trough below the infinity edge of the pool. She still nests nearby, and the couple has noticed a decrease in the dove and sparrow population in the neighborhood.

Maintenance is the key to the garden now. It takes a minimum of ten hours a week to keep up with trimming, pruning, deadheading, mowing, and hauling off debris. The Stewarts have some help, but they often clean up leaves with their walk-behind gas-powered vacuum called a Little Wonder. Magnolia and oak leaves have a shiny, slick surface that does not break down easily, so these leaves do not go into the compost heap. Mr. Stewart is in charge of cleaning the fountains and keeping up with all of the electrical work, equipment, and plumbing.

A daily walk-through helps keep the property in excellent shape. Dr. Stewart prefers to let some plants encroach upon the paths, lawn, and walls, but her husband likes a crisper look with clean edges. They have, of course, compromised quite well, and there is a good yin-and-yang effect throughout.

The pleasure they receive from the garden has unfolded over several years and is still unfolding. "It was fascinating to watch the plants grow in," says Mr. Stewart. "We actually decided to downsize many of the shrubs and trees we ordered because of the climate here. It is a very long growing season, and things grow quickly in a protected environment."

But it is the garden's seasonal changes that bring them the most joy. The pink 'Okame' cherry trees and azaleas burst into bloom in spring, followed by the magnolias with their huge flowers and lemony fragrance. The crape myrtles put on a summer display, and then their leaves turn shades of rust and orange and red for the fall, a season without much showy color in Charleston. Red maples blaze as late as January, so even in winter there is something to delight the senses.

FOR THE LOVE OF GARDENING

Mrs. Joseph H. (Peter) McGee is one of Charleston's premier gardeners. Seriously gardening since the 1980s when she became involved with the Garden Conservancy, Patti McGee, as she is known, has been the subject of numerous magazine articles and has received a major award from the Charleston Horticultural Society. Her gardens have been featured in two previous books by this author.

Intensely interested not only in plants but also in the people who love them, sell them, grow them, take care of, and share them, Mrs. McGee

The seating area under the porches lends itself to entertaining. The small pool is surrounded with a collection of succulents.

keeps abreast of the latest trends and discoveries. She is delighted by the rediscovery of an old-fashioned plant that has gone out of favor and can be introduced into her scheme. She loves to roam nurseries for plants with unusual texture, color, or blossoms and to give them a try among her constantly changing arrangements in the garden. She is more than willing to test a plant for a year or even more, and then ruthlessly dispose of it if it offends or does not perform well. A generous hostess, she serves coffee, tea, and cheese biscuits to her garden club while they listen to expert speakers and watch live demonstrations set up in her garden. While giving her own demonstration on planting pots, she offers some very good advice: "The bigger the pot, the better and don't get rid of those Styrofoam pieces that come in packaging; use them in the bottom of your pots for drainage and to keep down the weight of the pots, making them easier to move."

Just after moving to their present location in 1993, the McGees had a family wedding in the garden, and they had another one this past year. The process of getting the garden ready for the weddings provided just the sort of deadlines she thrives upon. Because she and her husband often entertain visiting gardening VIPs, Mrs. McGee tries hard to keep up her list of the plants in the garden; her guests are always asking questions about some of the unusual specimens she has collected. Fall is her favorite time of year, and she

A selection of plants sits on a garden table, ready to be put into the garden. The carriage house at the back overlooks a shady patio with a pool.

hard-prunes many of her plants in late July for a spectacular fall bloom. One of her greatest challenges is to have a beautiful garden in the spring when so many visitors come to Charleston, because she uses a lot of tender semitropicals, as well as tropicals that are protected in the winter and do not bloom until later in the year.

In October pink trumpet vine (*Podranea ricasoliana*) and baby blue plumbago, both natives of South Africa, bloom together in a tangle on the garden's fence along the street. The fence gets the southern sun, and the tender trumpet vine has managed to survive ever since Mrs. McGee acquired it many years ago at a sample booth during the Horticultural Society's annual

Fall color in the perennial garden bed comes from a mix of salvias, clerodendrums, ginger, and Mexican firespike. A dogwood lights up the background in subtle oranges and yellows.

plant sale and festival. Before the sasanquas and camellias add their soft pinks and reds, clerodendrums, blue ginger, salvias, and Mexican firespike add red, orange, yellow, and blue fall color to this nontraditional southern garden. "I never thought I would have so much red and yellow in the garden, but these strong colors work well here, and the hummingbirds are a bonus," she adds. Dozens of plants with unusual or contrasting textures are expertly arranged in every corner of the property. The live oak dominates, so smaller trees, such as the dogwood, are chosen with great care.

In the fall, after its bright orange waxy flowers have dropped, the pomegranate tree bears fruit, in spite of the many squirrels that flourish in the neighborhood. These omnipresent rodents are greatly attracted to the carefully pruned canopy of the live oak that dominates the garden and keeps most of it in filtered shade. Hellebores, ferns, elephant ears, Solomon's seal, and native azaleas are among the plants under its crown. As the tree has grown, so have the shade-garden plantings and the challenges that come with a lack of strong sunlight. Three shade plants that are particularly important are farfugiums, mahonias, and hellebores. "I just couldn't garden without them," states Mrs. McGee.

Inspired by her friend Ruth Knopf, an internationally known rosarian, Mrs. McGee drove to Thomasville, Georgia, to a specialty nursery and brought back twenty heritage roses in 1994. The oak tree, too much of a treasure to prune drastically, continued to stretch its limbs and steal the sun from the roses, slowing their growth and diminishing their bloom to the extent that only two have survived, 'Sombreuil' (1880) and the polyantha 'Perle d'Or' (1884). The former is a mildew-resistant hardy off-white climber, and the latter is a yellow blend that is quite fragrant. One of the trade-offs of having the oak tree, though, is being able almost to sit among its graceful branches when enjoying the second-story piazza of the Greek Revival house that overlooks the garden. The tree also provides much-needed summer shade as well as a roost for the handsome yellow-crowned night herons that occasionally make it their nesting place.

There are a few sunny spots, and growing succulents in these areas has become a new interest. Pots have always been featured in her gardens and collecting succulents has happily enabled Mrs. McGee to collect more containers.

One of many containers in the garden. This one is planted with lamium, candy tuft, alyssum, and variegated flax lily.

Mrs. McGee has always loved gardening and is particularly interested in the characteristics of individual plants. She started out inspired by friends and the knowledgeable gardeners she met as her fascination with gardening expanded. "At first," she confides, gesturing toward her large reference collection of gardening books and materials, "the White Flower Farm catalogue was my main textbook." She later went on to take classes at the New York Botanical Garden and to attend lectures and visit hundreds of gardens and dozens of plant nurseries. The annual plant festival sponsored by the Charleston Horticultural Society has always been a source of new material. She cherishes the lifelong friends she has made through gardening and the often serendipitous, always enriching experiences that occur when engaging with so many of the gardeners who have touched her life.

She feels strongly that gardening is a true art form; that all the elements important in painting—line, color, form, texture, negative and positive spaces, and composition—are also part of what makes a garden resonate. There is also the sculptural aspect of pruning, shaping, and forming the plants. Design and atmosphere also enter into the equation. And so does change. Climate, acts of God, growth of plants and neighborhoods, neglect, tree removal, building and renovation, a change in circumstance or focus, and many, many other variables make gardening one of life's most interesting challenges.

Plants in the Garden of Mrs. Joseph H. (Peter) McGee. In addition to hardy specimens of the plants most commonly grown in Charleston gardens, Mrs. McGee has collected varieties and cultivars that add depth, texture, color, and verticality to her carefully arranged and tended space.

Listed first are the trees, shrubs, and plants that thrive in the various shady and sunny spots of her garden. A list of the more unusual, rare, and tropical plants follows in each category. Annuals and succulents are generally not included, although many plants (not always in this garden) such as larkspur, *Melampodium,* four o'clocks, and even impatiens will reseed themselves in the Charleston climate.

Trees

Dogwood	Magnolia
Live Oak	Maple

Flowering and Evergreen Shrubs, Woody Plants, and Small Trees

Boxwood (more than six varieties and cultivars, including the dwarf cultivar 'Kingsville', as well as 'Beckett's Box')

Camellia japonica and *C. sasanqua*

Citrus × *meyeri* (Meyer lemon)

Danae racemosa (poet's laurel). Tolerant of both drought and deep shade, this slow-growing evergreen shrub eventually produces grape-size berries similar in color to the orange fruit of the loquat.

Daphne odora

Edgeworthia chrysantha (paper bush). The bark fibers from this plant are used to make the Japanese tissue paper frequently used in conservation. The shrub produces fragrant blossom clusters in spring before the leaves appear.

Fatshedera lizei 'Angyo Star' (tree ivy). Variegated. Creamy white and very pale yellow mixed with green.

Gardenia jasminoides (gardenia)

Hydrangea: There are at least seven different types in the garden and the list includes *H. arborescens* 'Annabelle'; *H. macrophylla* 'Ayesha'; 'Blue Wave'; 'Madame Emile Mouillere'; and 'Lemon Zest'; and *H. quercifolia* 'Snowflake'.

Illicium floridanum (anise shrub)

I. henryi (pink to red blooms, deer resistant)

I. mexicanum

I. parviflorum 'Florida Sunshine' (yellow or star anise)

Ilex crenata 'Sky Pencil'. Small and vertical, this holly adapts well to urban environments.

Justicia brandegeana (shrimp plant)

Laurel (sweet bay)

Mahonia aquifolium (Oregon grape). The mahonias are shade-tolerant evergreen shrubs producing fragrant yellow blossoms in early spring that are followed by beautiful blue berries. *M. japonica* was crossed with *M. lomariifolia* to produce *M. × media*. In addition to both of the parent plants, there are three cultivars of *M. × media* in the garden: 'Charity', which gets large; 'Lionel Fortescue', which blooms early and is said to have a lily-of-the-valley perfume; and 'Winter Sun', the smallest of the three. *M. eurybracteata* 'Soft Caress' is a wildly popular dwarf cultivar with pretty yellow blossoms.

Osmanthus americanus (wild olive, devilwood)

O. × Fortunei 'San Jose'. Introduced in 1941, this tea olive produces pale orange flowers from October through December.

O. fragrans (tea olive)

O. fragrans 'Aurantiacus'. The flowers are orange.

Plumbago

Podocarpus macrophyllus 'Maki'. Deer and sea-coast tolerant, this false yew's nickname is shrubby yew.

Podranea ricasoliana (pink trumpet vine)

Rhododendron (native azalea in gold, orange, and pink specimens)

Roses

Ruscus aculeatus (butcher's broom). Related to asparagus, this evergreen shrub got its name from the use of its sharp-spined branches to sweep butchers' blocks. It produces mildly toxic red berries, but other parts of the plant have medicinal properties, and the young shoots, when boiled, are a substitute for asparagus.

Sarcococca confusa (sweet box). Fragrant white blossoms and nearly black fruit are produced on this medium height shrub.

S. hookeriana. Similar to the species above, but considered deer-resistant.

Trachelospermum jasminoides (Confederate jasmine)

Perennials, Herbaceous Perennials, and Ferns

Acanthus mollis 'Summer Beauty'. This particular cultivar of "bear's breeches" is known for its heat tolerance. It will also tolerate a range of soil types as long as the soil is not often wet.

Ajuga reptans (bugleweed)

Arum italicum

Asarum splendens (Chinese wild ginger). A semi-evergreen that prefers moist soil.

Aspidistra crispa (crisp Chinese cast-iron plant). This plant has recently been introduced to the United States.

Aspidistra elatior. There are several cultivars of this hardy shade plant in the garden: 'Okame' is striped, and 'Spek-tacular' is a spotted introduction from local plantswoman Linda Guy.

Athyrium niponicum (Japanese painted fern)

Begonia. Like coleus, this is an extremely useful foliage plant that has many variants and is easily propagated.

Bletilla striata 'Albostriata' (hardy ground orchid)

Calanthe sieboldii (Japanese hardy ground orchid)

Coleus. There is a wide variety of this versatile plant that often winters over.

Colocasia (elephant ear)

Dianella (flax lily). Classified as an herb that is perennial in mild climates.

Disporum bodinieri 'Shina no tsuki' (China moon Solomon's seal)

Drimiopsis maculata (African false hosta). This spotted-leaf ground cover prefers dry shade and produces spikes of off-white bell-shaped flowers.

Eomecon chionantha (snow poppy). A very hardy plant that can be invasive.

Farfugium japonicum. Formerly known as *Ligularia,* this showy foliage plant with yellow daisylike blooms has a place of honor throughout the garden. Cultivars include 'Aureomaculatum', 'Argentea', 'Crispatum', 'Escargot', 'Last Dance', 'Giganteum', and 'Yaezaki', which has a double blossom.

Helleborus (numerous hybrids)

H. × hybridus 'Heronswood Double White'

H. foetidus 'Piccadilly'

H. orientalis 'Penny's Pink' (Lenten rose). Note: All parts of hellebores are toxic.

Hymenocallis (spider lily)

Indigofera (indigo)

Iris ensata (Japanese iris)

Iris fulva (copper iris). This reddish-brown iris performs well in wet soil. It is a Missouri native and is said to be pollinated by hummingbirds.

I. × *Louisiana*
I. pseudacorus. Yellow flowered and widespread in wet areas.
I. tectorum (wall iris)
I. unguicularis. The leaves are long and grasslike, and the plant has purple fragrant flowers.
Lamium maculatum (dead nettle)
Liriope muscari 'Big Blue'. This is a "workhorse" in the garden, according to Mrs. McGee.
L. muscari 'Pee Dee Ingot' (golden monkey grass)
Persicaria. The genus *Persicaria* was formerly classified in the genus *Polygonum.* Collectively known as smartweed, pink weed, or knotweed, many of the plants are highly invasive.
Polygonatum odoratum 'Variegatum' (striped Solomon's seal)
Polystichum polyblepharum (Korean tassel fern)
Rohdea japonica (sacred lily). The flowers are insignificant, but the dark green foliage grows well in deep shade.
Salvia. There are several varieties and cultivars in the garden, including *Salvia guaranitica* 'Black and Blue', *S. leucantha,* and *S. madrensis* 'Red Neck Girl'.
Scadoxus multiflorus (blood lily)
Sedum. A common and easily grown succulent of more than six hundred species.
Selaginella (spikemoss)
Talinum paniculatum 'Kingswood Gold' (jewels of Opar, fame flower)
Tricyrtis hirta 'Miyazaki' and 'Precious Metal' (toad lily)
T. ohsumiensis 'Lunar Eclipse'. The leaves are edged with white. Toad lilies spread easily and blend well with golden monkey grass.

Tropical and Subtropical Plants
Abutilon × *hybridum* (flowering maple). Summer tropical.
Clivia (Kaffir lily)
C. miniata (dwarf)
Dichorisandra thrysiflora (blue ginger)
Galphimia gracilis (also known as thryallis). A broadleaf evergreen with long-blooming yellow flowers.
Justicia fulvicoma (Mexican plume). *Hortus Third* describes this species of *Justicia* as similar to *J. brandegeana* but less ornamental, while several plant nurseries tout it as one of the showiest of the shrimp plants.
Odontonema strictum (Mexican firespike)
Plectranthus Strobilanthes (Persian shield)
Tibouchina (glory bush)
Xanthosoma. Foliage plant closely related to caladiums.

The garden seen from the driveway. The green wall and ball-topped pillars are actually clipped podocarpus.

THE GARDEN AT THE GEORGE MATTHEWS HOUSE (CA. 1743)

When dedicated preservationists and passionate gardeners acquired the Matthews house on Church Street in the heart of downtown Charleston, something magical occurred. The entire property is a showplace, much loved and enjoyed by its owners, their family and friends, and Donna and Bob Cox (Landscapes Limited), who installed and help maintain the garden.

Mr. and Mrs. Benjamin Lenhardt have always been gardeners, especially Mr. Lenhardt, who is chairman of the board of the Garden Conservancy and has also been on the board of the Chicago Botanic Garden. He worked in his grandmother's garden as a boy and sowed his first seeds in the red dirt of Charlotte, North Carolina.

The family was already living in the Historic District and enjoying a garden on King Street redesigned by Mr. Lenhardt when the opportunity arose

The formal entrance garden

to purchase the Matthews house. The house had always been in excellent hands but, over a period of almost three years of meticulous research and dedicated renovation, it was restored and altered to perfection. There were no traces of the Colonial garden except for a brick privy. There had been a garage at the end of the drive in the 1960s that was later demolished, along with a rectangular flower bed that ran the length of the free-standing two-story kitchen building.

The house, its slate roof, trims, picket fence, much of the paving materials, and most of its flowering plants are all variations of white and gray now, with subtle undertones of lavender, pink, and blue. The garden is enclosed and formal, but it includes small carefully planted areas that are more relaxed, providing interesting contrasts.

The plat was already well defined by the high facade of a pretty brick house on the southern lot line, the house and its kitchen building to the north, and walls and a fence enclosing the remainder of the property. Most of the walls were brick with some bare concrete block, which was painted a soft brown brick color prior to planting climbers. Carefully controlled vines and espaliered trees and shrubs were chosen not only to soften the borders but also to bring the garden down closer to eye level. Mr. Lenhardt planted tall hedges of Southern yew and low boxwood hedges to further define the separate areas, or rooms, of the garden.

He thoroughly enjoyed the design process. "I like photography and have taken thousands of pictures of gardens we have visited over the years. There are so many inspirational designs, but I did try to emulate the style of an English eighteenth-century parterre garden in the main area and in the small space in front of the house." The large group of ten beds planted with English and American boxwood, variegated ivy, and dwarf mondo grass (*Ophiopogon japonicus*) is overlooked by the porches, the kitchen building, and a seating area. The plantings and the patterns in these parterres have changed from his original sketches and choices because of plants' failure to thrive or failure to achieve the desired effect, but everything is growing well today.

The freshly painted ground-floor porch and driveway gates of the George Matthews House. Single-stem loquat trees line the drive opposite, and a potted palm adds a bit of privacy from the street for the main garden.

Local designs by Loutrel Briggs were another inspiration. Briggs frequently employed level changes to add another dimension. Several different materials were used for the hardscape. Crushed oyster shells worked well in the front garden, setting off the saturated greens of boxwood and *Rhaphiolepis*. The driveway was paved in pebble-dash with brick accent designs. Dark blue-gray slag was used for the paths between the pattern beds in the main garden, and flagstone paved the areas around the buildings. Old Charleston bricks formed borders, paths, and steps. Other types of stone and marble have been scattered about.

Just behind the kitchen building is an old privy with an orange tiled roof and a ball finial. The finial motif is repeated on top of a podocarpus (Southern yew) hedge clipped to resemble a wall with pillars and finials at the entrance to the far garden. This hedge runs at a right angle to the house and shelters the last of the garden rooms. Along the eastern side of the hedge are a white foxglove allée and a small area of plants with bold textures. There are also ginger lilies, white Japanese iris and white roses, begonias, and seasonal plants in this narrow bed. Planters full of an ever-changing variety of plants are strategically placed throughout. "My grandmother loved feverfew, and I have always had a bit of it in every one of my gardens," says Mr. Lenhardt.

At the far end of the property, along its western border, is the more private "Charleston" garden with its lawn and formal borders of holly, camellias, azaleas, and sasanquas. Included in the traditional plantings are crape myrtles, dogwood, tea olives, cleyera, viburnum, fatsia, and roses. Urns spill over with annuals in pastel colors, while the walls bloom with white roses,

The main garden view from the kitchen building

A white 'Lady Banks' rose spills over the southwest corner of the kitchen dependency. White lantana and white antique roses scramble up the walls. The espaliered magnolia in the middle is a 'Little Gem' cultivar.

The garden at dusk. The broken stone at the far left of the parterre garden is an old mooring post found buried near the privy. In the 1740s the house was at the edge of a creek.

An English-style garden bench provides shady seating at the far end of the garden.

The garden privy, beautifully restored, is used as a storage shed.

jasmine, *Solanum*, and clematis. An old camphor tree dominates one corner, and the curved limbs of a neighbor's live oaks filter the western sun.

Mr. Lenhardt believes gardening is one of the highest forms of artistic expression. The variables of weather, location, soil, choices of plant material and hardscape, time, and climate are just a few of the factors making it so fascinating, frustrating, and rewarding. Gardens are never static; they change daily and need constant care. "They are living art," he enthusiastically remarks.

Foxgloves, iris, and roses in the "cutting garden"

AN OLD CHARLESTON GARDEN

I loved this garden as a child. A classmate of mine and his brother lived in the house with its pretty fenced garden across the street from both my great-grandmother's and my great-aunt's houses. I remember attending ice cream parties on the porch, followed by storytelling. It was a lovely garden, a grown-up garden, but we were all welcome to use it as a yard for hide-and-seek or playing tag. And I adored the only large fountain in the neighborhood. It was lit up at night and made everything around it look romantic.

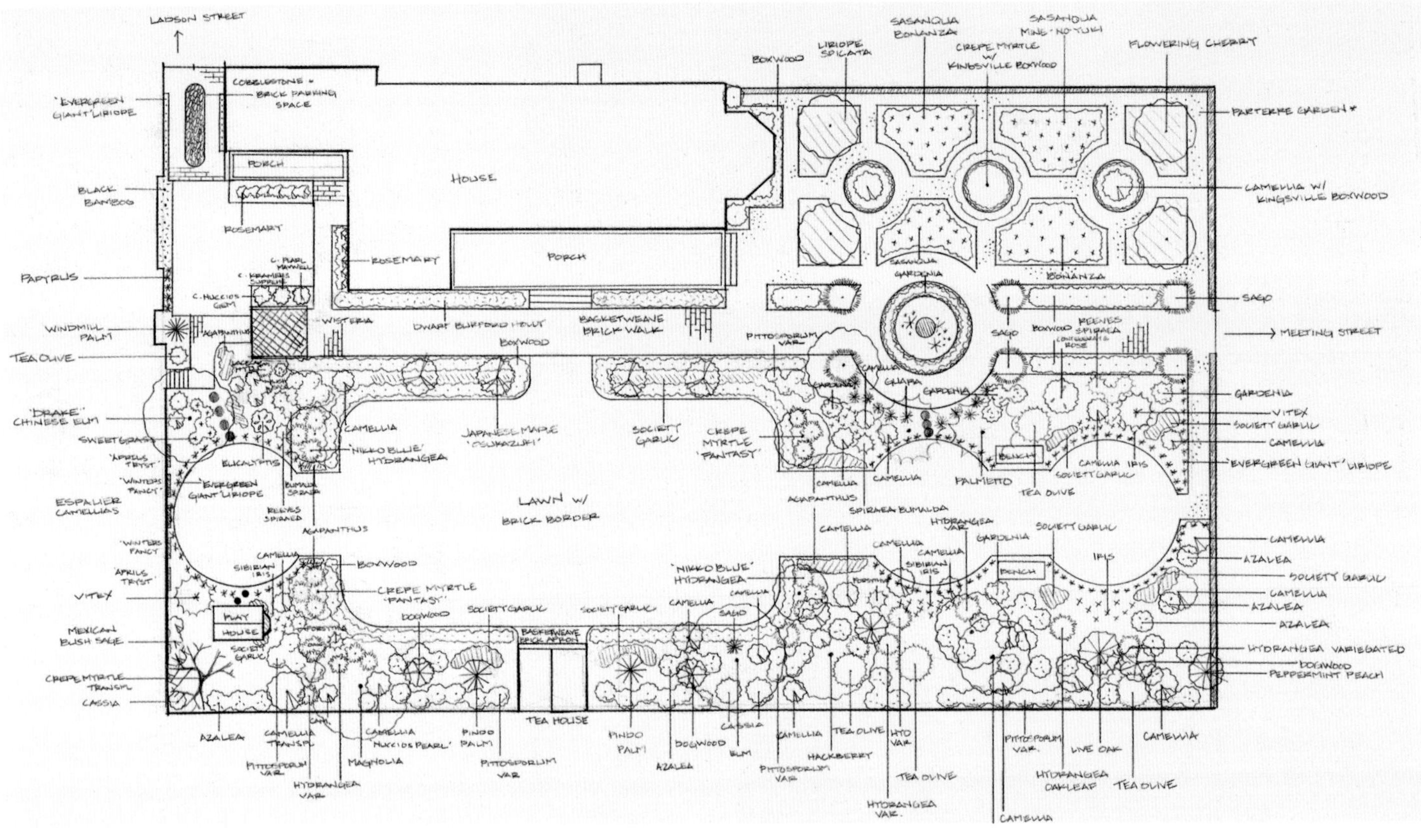

The current garden plan, drawn by Katy Wood. Courtesy of the owners.

It is still a very romantic place, and it remains in the family, who purchased it in the 1950s. The house, built circa 1792, has Victorian additions, including a bay window and a third story, and the garden also has late-nineteenth-century additions: a glorious fountain from Germany and a lattice-work garden folly that everyone calls the Tea House.

Working from a design based on nineteenth-century photographs, the owner's father lovingly laid out and planted the garden more than fifty years ago. Much time and effort were spent on an elaborate filter system for the old fountain's waterworks. The plant material was traditional and thrived, and then eventually became overgrown and exhausted. The next generation moved in, and their children and children's friends continued the pattern of playing in the big yard.

In 2005 the owners hired Katy Wood, a young horticulturist, to help refurbish and refresh the garden. They had admired the work Wood had done for neighbors and wanted her help especially in choosing blooming shrubs and trees that would provide color all year long and not require too much maintenance.

According to the owners, "Katy was a joy to work with, and her lovely landscape plan is framed and hanging in the front hall. The garden had good bones; it just needed fresh, good plants. And we wanted the garden to be structured but not too formal, as well as fun for entertaining." A particularly successful combination of colors occurs when the 'Fantasy' crape myrtles and the bluish-purple hydrangeas at the base of the trees bloom together. There are very few annuals, but there are traditional camellias, gardenias,

The Tea House viewed from the wisteria-covered arbor

azaleas, roses, spiraea, sasanquas, and tea olives for their flowers and fragrance. "I love this house," says its mistress. "It is not a grand house, but it relates beautifully to the garden; it just flows into it." They now use their garden mostly for entertaining, and will continue to do so until there is yet another generation of little boys who can happily dig holes in the yard and little girls who join them.

FACING The Victorian fountain in April with red buckeye, wisteria, and dogwood blooming in the background

A GARDEN IN THE OLD WALLED CITY

Charleston, along with Quebec City and Saint Augustine, Florida, was one of three walled cities along the east coast in the seventeenth and eighteenth centuries. Charleston's walls were completely taken down about 1740, the year in which a fire destroyed roughly 40 percent of the city's extant buildings. In the boundaries of the old walled city many of the rebuilt and surviving

Enormous tea olives give welcome shade to the patio. The tall hedges on either side are white azaleas bordered by boxwoods.

houses remained close up against each other on narrow lots. More buildings succumbed to another fire eight years later.

The William Bell House (ca. 1800) was built on the site of a previous structure presumably destroyed in the fire of 1748. This building was severely damaged by the earthquake of 1886, but it was repaired and still stands today. Major renovations occurred in the 1930s. Rumor has it that the stunning iron balcony added at that time was found in a local garage.

When the present owners bought the house more than twenty years ago, they completed more renovations, including an overhaul of the garden. A pair of tea olives (*Osmanthus fragrans*) heavily shaded a knot garden just

The fig vine on the garden shed is kept tightly clipped.

beyond the French doors leading outside from the house, and the plantings beneath them were not flourishing. In addition the garden from the 1950s had nearly disappeared: most of the long lot's surface had been paved with an assortment of material including orchard stone and slate.

There was little room for annuals, perennials, and bulbs. An open drain in the center of the pavement surrounded by six boxwoods caught run-off from the roof, and a small goldfish pool without a drain was no longer decorative. The owners found a dedicated mason who procured a cache of old brick, extended the slightly raised terrace in place of the knot garden, and built a low wall enclosing it. The new terrace was perfect for dining and entertaining outdoors and provided a shady place for viewing the garden through the arch formed by the fifty-year-old tea olives. The wall was made wide enough for seating and also to accommodate the pair of lion statues that had reigned over their pretty garden when they lived in London.

Paving was removed to make room for flowerbeds at the three perimeters of the sunny far end of the walled-in garden, and the little pool was filled in. An old photograph of the back of the house shows that there was a lawn before the mixed stone paving was installed. The family briefly considered putting in grass. Their next-door neighbor, who had a well-known garden, nodded slowly upon being consulted, puffed on his pipe, and stated,

The view of the house from the garden

"Well, some people have *tried.*"

There were hardy white azalea hedges symmetrically planted along the central part of the garden. Set off by lower boxwood hedges, these were lovely in the spring and were retained. The walls on either side of the remainder of the property, however, seemed bare and somewhat forlorn. The solution was to plant fig vine and hollies and to build a support frame for Confederate jasmine and a 'Lady Banks' rose to be planted by the terrace. Citrus trees in big terra-cotta pots against the house not only produce fruit, but are fragrant and decorative as well, especially with a changing variety of colorful annuals at the base of the trees' stems.

As part of a practice of prudent gardening, the soil was tested and amended. Hydrangeas were put in for cool summer and fall color; different varieties of lilies were added as accents; and the central area containing the drain was disguised by ground covers, a tall container of cascading ferns, and several curved cast-iron benches. A *Magnolia* × *soulangiana* provided a partial focal point from the terrace but was later enhanced by the climbing single white Cherokee rose and a pale yellow 'New Dawn' climber. The ramblers give privacy to a table and chairs frequently used for alfresco meals. One year when the children were all together, the family had Christmas dinner in the garden.

The owners modestly insist that they "just touched the garden here and there." Changing and adding new plants every year is much of the fun of it for the couple, who frequently remark that they are so fortunate to be able to enjoy such a wonderful spot in such a delightful city.

A GARDEN OF QUIET CONTRASTS

The house had tremendous appeal: it dated from the first quarter of the twentieth century and had Italianate overtones, but the potential for the garden made the sale. The lot was long and narrow and very deep. Suzanne Haythe

White roses cover the fence in front of the house.

The curve in the bed planted with a fan palm allows just an enticing peek at the garden beyond.

and her husband knew that they wanted it to be paved and full of plants with texture and interesting shapes.

Dr. E. G. Johnson, a retired radiologist and garden designer, was hired to come up with a plan that would reflect the sophisticated and quiet style of the owners. He drew a series of garden rooms, each of which had its own character, but all of which worked together in a completely paved corridor leading to a raised random ashlar stone patio at the very end of the property. Robert Johnson, a talented brick mason, helped design and execute the

The vibrant colors of crape myrtles fill the garden in early summer after the white *Cercis* have finished blossoming.

bluestone, brick, and ashlar stone paving in a pleasing and interesting range of patterns, beginning with the driveway.

The main entrance to the garden is through the house and its porches, but the narrow parking area is beautifully incorporated into the design. It is well planted with hardy shade plants and leads to a handsome wooden gate that also accesses the garden. Lime trees in large lime-colored glazed pots stand opposite a pair of flowering cherry trees just behind the gate. A curved bed containing a gorgeous fan palm conceals the garden rooms and the surprising length of the garden. The first room mimics a courtyard. Four formal beds outlined with boxwoods each contain a white redbud (*Cercis canadensis* 'Alba') underplanted with white 'Iceberg' roses. The redbuds, which are cold-hardy up to USDA zone 5, have bronze new leaves that turn green in summer and yellow in the fall. "It looks like there's been a snowfall when

Sunlight begins to warm a teak bench surrounded by Confederate jasmine.

they blossom in early spring," says Mrs. Haythe. "This is not a garden full of unusual things, but I do love going to the nurseries." There is an unusual flourish, however, in the center of the four beds: an enormous clay vessel is surrounded by a circular boxwood hedge. It lends an exotic touch. A seating area just off the courtyard has three amusing theatrical masks arranged above a teak bench that sits in a sunny southern exposure surrounded by fragrant Confederate jasmine.

Color in the garden is subtle until the crape myrtles put on their summer show. Most of the plants have white or pale flowers: white roses, oak leaf and limelight hydrangeas, gardenias, citrus trees, viburnum, and *Acanthus*. Mrs. Haythe also loves cool blues and enjoys iris, agapanthus (lily of the Nile), hydrangeas, and plumbago for their various shades of blue to lavender. Olive bushes, prostrate *Taxus*, camellias, sasanquas, palms, daphne, elephant ears (*Colocasia*), variegated flax, pittosporum, and a variety of ferns not only add texture but also display the many shades of green so appealing to the owners. The shrubs, boxwoods, and trees have flourished over the five years since their installation. As Dr. Johnson remarked, "Most of the plants are traditional ones for Charleston and work exceptionally well."

Detail of artwork on the pool painted by Carl Beckwith Smith

Mrs. Haythe wanted water in her garden, and she and Dr. Johnson agreed on a long oval pool in the third and largest space that is divided from the courtyard by podocarpus (Southern yew) hedges. Inspired by visits to many sites, she decided to pave the bottom with cobblestones, visible through the shallow clear water. When completed, the stark concrete sides of the pool seemed to need decoration. Carl Beckwith Smith, a local artist and trompe l'oeil limner, painted a soft green and terra-cotta pattern around the exterior that was inspired by the designs on a pair of Spanish pots already in the garden.

Mrs. Haythe felt that another architectural element was needed to add interest and imported a charming little wood and glass folly from Norfolk, England. It has a bell-curve slate roof with a ball on the top and provides shelter with a view. It is nestled in the wide shady shrubbery under the crape myrtles on the southern aspect of the long garden. At the end of the garden steps lead to a patio nicknamed "the stage," where there is seating and an umbrella for shade. The change in elevation is an important element in the design. Fortunately, the background of the stage is the side of a neighboring eighteenth-century brick outbuilding. A mature oak on the property line at the far southern edge and a mature *Magnolia grandiflora* just over the line give a sense of grandeur and, at the same time, a feeling of enclosure and privacy.

Mrs. Haythe explains that she is "very visual," and, although she wants abundant growth in her garden instead of multiple "itsy-bitsy" plants, she realizes that the garden's success is due to form and simplicity. Green and white dominate most of the year. "There's a formality to the garden, and yet it is uncomplicated, simple, and fresh."

A TRADITIONAL SMALL GARDEN

Tucked away on a narrow street in the Historic District is a much-loved garden that has been designed and redesigned by professionals to work within narrow confines and to provide variety and interest for its owners.

The present owner, a serious gardener, bought the property in 2011 and has been adding her personal touches ever since. She gardens daily. The *Farmer's Almanac* and local nurserymen are predicting a cold winter, she

A brick path in a herringbone pattern leads from the front door straight to the garden gate. Ginger lilies (*Hedychium coronarium*) edge the wall, and apricot hibiscus plants bloom on the right.

The garden lawn seen from the house in early summer

reports, so when I met with her on an August afternoon, she was already contemplating ways to protect the tender semitropicals that had flourished over the past summer and previous warm winter.

A narrow walk between walls leads to the garden gate and doubles as parking space for skilled drivers. It is paved with a variety of brick and bluestone that changes patterns as it leads through the garden to the front door. Along this path, ginger lilies bloom in late summer and early fall against an old brick wall to the right.

To the left as you enter is a zoysia lawn, once described as having the shape of a hurricane glass globe, anchored at the street end with a small patio furnished with cast-iron garden chairs and tables. This seating area faces a charming statue of a smiling Pan playing his pipes and spilling water into a little pond of goldfish. A quartet of potted hibiscus marks the corners of the space.

The hidden courtyard is only a few feet wide.

At the house end is a wooden pergola with more seating, including benches and a chaise longue. White clematis and mandevilla are trained on the supports to help provide shade. Connecting the lawn to the patios is a ten-foot-long brick wall to the north that used to be covered with a tangled mass of vines. "The wall was so handsome that I wanted it exposed," says our gardener. "It has color, texture, and history.

"I chose a 'Little Gem' magnolia to espalier in the middle and put decorative iron pieces on either side for training roses and blooming vines." Beds of clipped boxwood and other shrubs, with space for annuals and bulbs, formally edge the lawn and make the garden seem much larger than it is. Two white crape myrtle trees soften the walls and the skyline.

With a background in managing retail stores, the owner counts design as a skill that translates naturally into the landscape of the garden. She loves balance, proportion, color, and texture. She always starts with white and adds color at her whim. Right now the garden has many apricot and pink accents, but blues and purples are always popular. Pots are her favorite decorative pieces. There are huge sand-colored glazed pots of junipers that give extra privacy to the area under the pergola; tall neutral green pots with conical ivy topiaries on either side of the front door; glazed pots filled with boxwood balls at the gate; and a myriad of smaller pots of different heights and colors artistically placed throughout, many planted with herbs for the kitchen. Greens are carefully chosen in a wide variety of plant materials with different shades and textures. Ivy trained into globes, cones, and spirals is a mainstay.

A hidden courtyard that is not much more than ten-by-twenty feet lies behind the house. It contains a wall fountain flanked by a pair of maroon glazed pots that are planted with birds of paradise. Fig vine (*Ficus pumila*) is trained on a pair of trellis-work wire squares on the white stucco wall that marks the end of the property. This intimate area has a more casual feel, and the ferns and plants spill out of hanging pots and other planters in multiple colors and textures.

Small trees in pots give added privacy to the seating area at the front of the house. Vines will cover the loggia by late summer.

Much of the plant material is traditional and sturdy: there are sasanquas, jasmine vines, fatsias, *Aspidistra,* boxwoods, papyrus, ligustrum, roses, and hydrangeas. But there are also blue podocarpus shrubs, birds of paradise, and orchids that need to be protected in winter. The green and white sun-tolerant caladiums will be replaced with snapdragons this year, with old-fashioned fragrant stock and pansies in front of the snaps. "I never seem to get the garden exactly the way I want it," says its steward, "but the garden is such a joy to me, and I am driven to continue creating and shaping it."

Gardens Farther Afield

A COLLECTION OF TROPICALS

A garden frequently reflects the personalities and tastes of its stewards, and this gem on James Island is no exception. The vibrant and talented artists, photographers, and businessmen James Smeal and Alejandro

A traditional boxwood-lined grass path sets off hundreds of tropical plants.

Gonzalez have created a masterpiece of color and texture along a lowcountry marsh.

Their canvas was an abandoned property of about one and one-third acres. The house had burned; the traditional plantings of azaleas, camellias, and ligustrum were completely overgrown beneath live oaks in need of pruning; and there was no longer any structure or plan to the arrangement of what was once a garden.

Starting over, the new owners rebuilt the house using some of the walls and the foundation in a "Floridian or island" style, as they call it, with arches and windows for enjoying the views and breezes. The roof and eaves were washed in turquoise paint to establish the informal, lighthearted feel of the new establishment. Then gardening began in earnest.

Alejandro Gonzalez rooted hundreds of cuttings and established ligustrum hedges along the entrance drive that swoop and arch and thrust upward into a series of well-defined squares. This touch of whimsy is the introductory note to the playfulness seen in the rest of the garden.

The plan formed slowly. The property is surrounded by beautiful mature live oaks, tall pines, and a few hardwoods and evergreens, so the eye is drawn up and around. Jim Smeal had the idea of camouflaging some of the pruning scars on the oaks with plants and got out the big ladders. Now some branches high up in the trees are used as bases for displays of bromeliads, ferns, and mosses. Epiphytes and aerophytes are artfully arranged on the trunks as well, especially on the rough surfaces and crannies of the palms.

Grassy or mulched paths meander through the entire garden in a rough circle around the house. At the entrance the house protects masses of colorful mixed bromeliads from chilly wind. During the coldest weeks a temporary cold frame is constructed from bamboo poles and plastic. The bromeliad collection, a favorite of these two gardeners for its variety, toughness, and brilliant color, is often enhanced by annual trips to specialty nurseries in Florida. Hundreds of plants have been brought in over the past decade and hundreds more have been propagated. The small lawn area surrounded by the huge display of bromeliads is punctuated by a simple large terra-cotta fountain vase in the middle of a low liriope (monkey grass) planting.

One of many artful plantings of colorful tropicals. Bromeliads were placed along the high oak branch in the background.

Farfugium (formerly called *Ligularia*), both spotted and variegated, all sorts of ferns, grasses, tuberous begonias, philodendrons, cannas, aloes, dahlias, and palms add to the highly textured character of the deep beds that have grown larger over the years. Beyond the entrance the lawn expands and sweeps down to the marsh and the live oaks at its edge. Here the plantings are kept simple. Hydrangeas bloom near the house starting in June. In the spring the original azaleas still bloom, but these are nearly covered by lush growth each summer, as are the winter-blooming camellias. A narrow path bordered by interesting plants leads through the marsh out to a circular spit of high ground where there is a spectacular view of the water and seating from which to enjoy it.

As the lawn comes back around to the house, there is a slope to the far right where variegated liriope is planted in a series of crescents ending in a leaf-shaped double crescent: a living sculpture. The grass path then leads through an allée of Italian cypresses underplanted with hydrangeas, daylilies, and a variety of tropicals. A Chinese parasol tree (*Firmiana simplex*) dominates the last of the small rooms veering off from the main path.

There is an enormous variety of plants in the series of rooms of this fascinating garden, all unified by a common thread of bright color and the tropical feel of this pocket of creativity. *Eryngium* (sea holly), *Elaeagnus*,

Lilies and white hydrangeas bloom among other plantings at the marsh's edge.

Crescents of variegated liriope decorate the lawn at one of the edges of the property, delineated by the hedge in the background.

A swath of lawn sets off the beauty of live oaks along the edge of the marsh.

Bromeliads have been carefully placed on this live oak tree.

A large aechmea has bright red stems.

Euphorbia, ginger lilies, fennel, ornamental grasses, amaryllis lilies, red hot poker plant (*Kniphofia uvaria*), bougainvillea, yucca, mahonias, cassias, many succulents, beschornerias, begonias, aloes, agaves, bananas, citrus trees, palms, plumerias, serrissas, wild olive, golden rain tree (*Koelreuteria paniculata*), and tung oil tree (*Aleurites fordii*) are all at home here. Hanging baskets host interesting arrangements and plants with character, such as *Sedum morganianum* (burro's tail).

Wildlife also populates the garden. There are songbirds, herons, egrets, snakes, possums, raccoons, and squirrels. There used to be a population of marsh rats and other small rodents, but the black racers and the garter snake

The cypress allée

that lives in the attic have done a good job of controlling them. Some of the owners' favorite creatures among the plants and trees are the box turtles and the small owls. There was once a fox who roamed through occasionally.

This is a much-enjoyed and cared for environment that not only delights the gardeners' eyes and other senses but also stimulates the mind. "It is constantly changing and evolving," says Jim Smeal, "and I am still learning so much. I love the garden for that gift."

A COUNTRY GARDEN IN THE CITY

Twenty years ago, when the young family (an engineer, his wife, and their children) found nearly two acres for sale in the middle of the West Ashley area of Charleston, they were delighted with the property. It had a comfortable house, several storage buildings, a playhouse, room for the dogs and children to run, and plenty of space to add porches, a pool, and a patio.

Previous owners had been very interested in the landscape, as their degrees were in horticulture, botany, and zoology. However, it had been many

Potted plants are displayed in two of the seating areas near the swimming pool. The bright yellow-green shrub in the background is *Ligustrum sinense*, and the striking red palmlike plant to the right is a *Cordyline australis*.

years since the property had been properly gardened. The new owners, also gardeners, had a lot of work ahead.

There were lovely trees everywhere. Pecan, sweet gum, mulberry, maple, live oak, dogwood and holly grew on the lot, as well as a mature Virginia pine and a huge bald cypress that had been planted near the entrance. A beautiful old camellia collection also graced the remnants of the old garden. Running bamboo, however, had nearly taken over the acre behind the house. Undaunted, the owners hired help and rented a chipper. Their estimate is that more than forty thousand stalks of the invasive bamboo were cut and shredded.

Today there is a framework of reliable and handsome trees and plants that outline and punctuate the property, with more unusual and trial plants scattered throughout. The overall design is one of deep flower beds around and along a lawn that embraces the house in the middle. From the left side of the house, the grass swoops up a small hill created from the dirt left over from the pool installation and around another berm across the back of the garden. It then leads past a shady protected area used as a nursery for propagating and storing plants, a vegetable garden, and a parking area, and then back around to the entrance and semicircular drive.

The pool is located directly behind the dwelling within a formal design. Crape myrtles punctuate symmetrical boxwood-lined beds at the house end and provide shade for an open verandah. At the other end of the pool the same patterns of boxwoods enclose sun-loving plants, and a well-maintained hedge of southern magnolias screens the back of the property and neighboring houses from view. Paths veer off to several seating areas surrounded by beds of favorite plants and pots full of color.

The owners love trees and have the luxury of space to allow them to grow as specimens. Many new trees have been planted in the past years. The fringe tree (*Chionanthus retusus*) that produces masses of delicate white flowers can grow up to twenty feet high and just as wide. The isu tree (*Distylium racemosum*) is a small tree in cultivation, but it can grow up to eighty feet in its native areas of Japan, China, and the Himalayas. It has a red flower in the spring. *Isu* means "chair" in Japanese, and the wood is used for making furniture and art objects. Japanese maples also enhance the garden, as do several cultivars of *Magnolia grandiflora*.

The purple spikes of the chaste tree shed raindrops in front of a background of hydrangeas.

There's a lacebark elm, also known as the Chinese elm, and a single longleaf pine tree lives in a pot. A chaste tree (*Vitex agnus-castus*) by the house has purple spiky blooms in the summer. Big old-fashioned garden figs produce enough fruit for the birds and the family. Palmettos and pindo palms mix in well with the hardwoods, evergreens, and flowering trees.

There is a touch of the romantic in the garden. A "secret" path along the perimeter is shaded by overhanging tree branches and hidden by shrubbery. At the crest of the smallest berm, there is a grass circle with a ring of stones in the center and rustic chairs for seating. This is the "Council Ring," inspired by the work of the western landscape architect Jens Jensen. The grassy path continues through an unusual allée of Brodie cedars (*Juniperis virginiana* 'Brodie Cedar') and down behind a man-made mound that hides the house from view.

Shrubs are everywhere and quite varied. There are blue, pink, and white hydrangeas, three varieties of viburnum (*Viburnum odoratissimum* var. *awabuki*, *V. odoratissimum*, and *V. tinus*), southern and native azaleas, quite a few unidentified camellias, *Eurya japonica* (related to the camellia), gardenias, banana shrubs (*Michelia figo*), beautyberry (*Callicarpa americana*), roses, *Ligustrum sinense*, Chinese quinine (*Dichroa*), and a *Daphniphyllum*.

Against the background of shrubs throughout, including previously well established ligustrum hedges, there are dedicated flower beds with a wide assortment of annuals, perennials, bulbs, roses, ground covers, and grasses. Crinum lilies, crocosmias, irises, red ginger, salvias, ferns, farfugium, and succulents are included in the mix. One particularly colorful bed is planted to attract butterflies, another to display unusual or rare plants.

"When we were first clearing the property and drawing out plans, I used to think that the emphasis in the garden should be on structure," points out one of the owners. "Then I started collecting plants, and now I have a 'garden of excess,'" she laughs. "But it is a garden for strolling and pleasure, and I love spending entire days immersed in the work and the enjoyment of it."

An urn on a pedestal planted with a succulent adds formality and a touch of whimsy to one of the lawns.

The cool blues and lavenders of hydrangeas mix with a variety of shrubs beneath a crape myrtle near the pool.

A GARDEN SANCTUARY ON JAMES ISLAND

Three years ago, when Patricia Harpell moved into her little white house on James Island, she pulled into the driveway with an eighteen-foot U-Haul trailer spilling over with plants from Massachusetts. Of course most of the plants could not tolerate the Charleston area's heat and humidity, but this experienced gardener was undaunted.

The lot was nearly one-third of an acre and had almost full sun. There were a few crape myrtle trees, a palm or two, a healthy chest-high ligustrum hedge, and large azaleas planted around the foundations of the house. The lawn was spotty. Starting with a nearly clean palette, she arranged hoses in pleasing curves to mark the bed outlines and started gathering large amounts of scrap cardboard and newspapers from the recycling center.

Using a process called "sheeting," she laid down layers and layers of the cardboard and paper to kill the grass and weeds and to form the basis of the flowerbeds. Jeff Tant of Full Circle Gardens and Landscapes was hired to bring in more than twenty-four tons of compost to go on top of the sheeting and to help with some of the heaviest gardening chores. The compost was a key element, as the soil was severely depleted.

Then the fun began in earnest. Just as the garden was taking shape, neighbors down the street began renovating and removed all of their foundation plantings. Mrs. Harpell drove her car there and, with the neighbors'

Roses climb on the arch over one of the main garden paths. In late October the cornlike growth of purple pearl millet, orange and yellow coleus, heather, fuzzy purple *Salvia leucantha*, and pots of succulents line the walkway where Isabella the cat has spotted something interesting.

full permission, began hauling mature plants back to her property. Admiring her determination, the family brought the entire mass of greenery to their new friend on a flatbed truck.

The garden is loosely organized into sections around the house, which sits on a corner lot. In front of the house to the northeast and west, masses of woody perennials, roses, ornamental grasses, salvias, purple pearl millet, bottlebrush bushes, and dozens of semitropicals such as cannas, bananas, and ginger mingle in a colorful mélange. Butterflies, hummingbirds, bluebirds, and songbirds are in nearly constant attendance. Tea olives, pittosporum, crape myrtles, magnolias, maples, and palm trees are interspersed in a roughly structured pattern. In addition to the grassy paths that wind around the overflowing beds, there are two paved walkways leading to the house, each punctuated by a series of metal arches covered in climbing roses and vines.

To the southeast in front of the house, a raised-bed vegetable garden surrounded by peach, olive, fig, pear and kumquat trees and berry bushes is also home to several compost heaps and an assortment of potted succulents, *alocasia* (elephant ears), cuphea, and nasturtiums. A trellis supports

A pair of glossy magnolias will eventually shade this sunny area. The mounding plant with orange flowers is lantana.

Luffa (loofah) vines that produce sponges much-used by the household. The southern aspect of the lot holds fragrant shrubs such as *Aloysia* (verbena family) and a delightful assortment of unusual plants. There are blooming toad lilies, the succulent furcraea, *Verbena bonariensis,* big leaf begonias, *heliconia, Odontonema,* ground covers, *Thunbergia grandiflora* with its blue trumpet flowers, and various citrus trees, all overlooked by a small outdoor cooking area. Quite a few plants in the garden have been rescued from trash piles and are thriving in their new environment.

The western side garden at the back of the house is completely shaded during all but the winter months by an enormous hackberry on a

An unusual gate marks the entrance to the shade garden.

A bright combination of colors and textures lights up a small area.

neighboring lot. The area used to be used for dog pens and is now home to hellebores, Solomon's seal, *Farfugium* with its beautiful round leaves, unusual and common ferns, and more of the owner's favorite rex begonias.

Patricia Harpell is a practicing herbalist who teaches traditional herbalism. She recently started the South Carolina Herbal Society. Her garden is organic, and she is strict about not using pesticides or other chemicals. Her herb garden sits on the northern side of the house for its southern exposure, between a pair of wooden arbors supporting scuppernong and muscadine grape vines. A whimsical white birdhouse covered in a passion vine marks the center of the garden and has attracted nesting bluebirds for two years. Noisette roses form a border along the street. There is, of course, a wide variety of useful herbs in the beds, as well as the mystical white sage and other aromatics. Patricia Harpell makes elderberry syrup for the elder flowers she dips and cooks in pancake batter; she brews herbal teas; grape leaves are preserved for later use in dolmades, a Greek delicacy; arugula and other greens grown in this protected spot are used in salads; and the berries of the *Vitex* shrub are ground to a powder that is a natural rooting hormone.

With her natural 'green thumb' and passion for growing all plants, Mrs. Harpell has transformed an ordinary suburban lot into an imaginative, functional, and productive garden bursting with color, texture, and the enthusiasm of its creator.

A GARDEN OF SUCCULENT DELIGHTS

Gardening with unusual plants has become Amy Johnson's passion. In 1986, when she and her husband moved to a one-story home in West Ashley, he volunteered to "do the yard," and soon part of the irregular lot was enclosed

Crushed rock, river stones, and containers
in the front garden

with a wooden fence for keeping in the dog. Not much happened for a couple of years, so Mrs. Johnson bought enough red-tips and privets, including ligustrums, to form solid hedges. She discovered George Hyams's wonderful nursery on James Island and ordered a few maple trees, which Hyams's staff planted for her.

The lot, however, flooded in heavy rain and the maples declined due to too much standing water. She started thinking about the problem and turned to books on design and gardening for a solution. Her background in art and her love of modern architecture made it easy to immerse herself in

A collection and arrangement of succulents and air plants in a large container

the designs of Frank Lloyd Wright and Richard Neutra and then in the landscaping around many of their buildings.

Amy Johnson grew up in Charleston, but her family's garden had no azaleas, camellias, or dogwoods. Her grandmother, the daughter of the Morris Island Lighthouse keeper, and her grandfather owned a plant shop that specialized in cacti. Many years later, when her grandmother died, her grandfather and his plants moved in with her parents. Her childhood garden was full of colorful Mexican pots, donkey carts, and prickly plants.

Design books provided a plethora of ideas for container gardening. She decided to elevate the front garden with three enormous "woks," purchased at Hyams Garden & Accent Store, and chose Mexican Grass Trees (*Dasylirion longissimum*) for the planters. The slender leaves grow to about six feet and provide year-round interest. Immediately, a rhythm was established. Crushed rock eventually replaced muddy patches and helped with drainage, river rocks and small boulders added more texture, and a collection of colorful pottery and plants began in earnest.

There was a garage in the back yard and a neighborhood refuse pile behind the garage. The area was a dirt patch that was heavily shaded by two magnolias and populated by dozens of rabbits. Mrs. Johnson continued to consult her books and designers: Billy Baldwin (who thought of himself primarily as a colorist), Debra Lee Baldwin (on succulents), Thomas Hobbs (*The Jewel Box Garden*), and Zahid Sardan (*New Garden Design*) were among the most inspirational.

Fanciful glass art is placed in pots and in beds.

FACING The path leading to the deck is bordered with more pots full of exotics and unusual specimens.

The garden slowly emerged as the Johnsons built decking at the back of the house and a smaller deck behind the garage that overlooked a koi pond. Changes in elevation added interest and rearranged focal points. Mrs. Johnson's fascination with plants became, in her words, "a beautiful, interspersed presentation on a small scale."

She subscribed to *Garden Design* magazine, attended garden shows, ordered hard-to-find plants from specialty nurseries, and found interesting containers and objects to decorate her outdoor arrangements. Against a background of traditional hard-working local plants, she experimented with dozens of agaves, aloes, bromeliads, cacti, dyckias, echeverias, euphorbias, sedums, senecios, and tillandsias, learning what worked best in each location. She blends the traditional with the unusual, delighting in the intermingling and combination of different plants' textures, colors, and shapes. Sometimes the planning goes awry, as specific material is unavailable or does not thrive as expected, but there are also serendipitous surprises. There are few annuals. Most plants are hardy and are decorative all year long, although some tender specimens need to be brought inside if a freeze is predicted.

Mrs. Johnson recently hired Jason Travis to build an elaborate and elegant privacy fence of wood and lacquered bamboo that sets an oriental tone around most of the property. There's a barbeque grill surrounded by large, colorful pots of colorful plants such as 'Sticks of Fire' (*Euphorbia tirucalli*), with a "floating" fabric roof nearby for protection from sun and mist. Glass ornaments augment the garden and catch the light. She has filled in the koi pond and added more hardscape and pots, and construction of an arbor is planned for the future. Eclectic, whimsical, and full of energy, this garden reflects its keeper's personality. Mrs. Johnson loves the fact that it is her artistic outlet and hopes that it may inspire others to be creative as well.

An unusual feature in the lowcountry, a waterfall cascades down the bluff.

A GARDEN WITH A WATERFALL

"I have always wanted to live here," says the gardener, who has also enjoyed living in a family home downtown and in a home on one of the sea islands near Charleston. She and her husband bought the house with about two acres of land on James Island a little more than ten years ago, and they absolutely love it. The house was not built until after Hurricane Hugo in 1989, and the huge oak trees and much of the plant material on the lot had been badly damaged by the storm. The lot had also been subdivided, and the first enormous job the owners tackled was to hire a landscape architect to draw up plans for enclosing the space with tall dark-green fencing that would give privacy and be a handsome backdrop for trees and shrubs.

When Paul Mulkey, a local arborist and landscaper, was hired to prune and feed the live oaks, they liked his ideas and enthusiasm about the property, and the trio has been working together successfully now for several years. Mulkey cleared the scrub and brush beneath the trees in the spacious entrance to the property, making room for hydrangeas and other shade plants. The driveway was redirected into a circle, and paths leading to areas of interest were established.

At the entrance to the house a riot of color and a small fountain introduce the garden and its surprises beyond. A dry river bed of dark gray cobbles runs along the building to its right; to the left are a full outdoor kitchen and a seating area with a fire pit.

The view through the house, from its rooms, balconies, decks, and porches, is spectacular. Up on a high bluff, the property overlooks the Intracoastal Waterway and the marshes along its edge. Plants are everywhere. "I inherited my love of plants and color from my mother, who grew up in the country and always had a pretty flower garden," she says. "I also enjoy flower arranging and grow many shrubs just for that purpose."

The most surprising element of the cliff is the rock-lined waterfall that cascades down to a lower deck. This area contains a fireplace and low walls for seating in addition to lounge and deck chairs. An outdoor dining room with a roof provides shade and protection from the rain, as does the small roof over a section of the walkway to the dock. Large colorful glazed pots contain red Australian bottlebrush trees (*Callistemon rigidus*) and other tropicals. Contrasting colors are a hallmark, especially shades of chartreuse, red, orange, and purple.

The owners wanted to make their home a welcoming and fun place for family and friends, so the emphasis is on entertaining in a garden setting. They have hosted family weddings and engagement parties and love having grandchildren play under their watchful eyes. But the mistress of the property admits that she always wanted a secret garden. Now a hidden shady path winds among tall shrubs and ends at a small seating area with a soft burbling fountain and an arbor covered in Confederate jasmine, making a quiet and spiritual space for reflection, meditation, and reading.

Lavender acanthus and orange impatiens bloom in the secret garden.

House Museum Gardens

The Charleston Museum, Historic Charleston Foundation, and Middleton Place Foundation each maintain one or more museum houses on the peninsula. These are the Joseph Manigault House, the Heyward Washington House, the Aiken-Rhett House, the Russell House, and the Edmondston-Alston House. The Calhoun Mansion and a small house on Church Street are privately owned but are open to the public. Most of the houses have pretty gardens that are also on view. At Christmas the Garden Club of Charleston beautifully decorates the Joseph Manigault House with greenery, flower arrangements, and historically accurate trimmings and decorations.

The gate house to the Joseph Manigault House on Meeting Street has been decorated for Christmas.

THE HEYWARD-WASHINGTON HOUSE

George Washington came to Charleston in May 1791, making the long journey down south from Philadelphia on horseback. For his much-anticipated visit, the City of Charleston rented a house on Church Street. Now called the Heyward-Washington House, it is owned by the Charleston Museum, and the formal garden, with its preserved outbuildings that include a kitchen and a privy, is maintained by the Garden Club of Charleston. An effort is made to grow only the types of plants and the actual plants that were known to be popular prior to General Washington's visit. The general did not remark on the city's gardens in his diary, but did note that in April of 1971, he "was visited about 2 o'clock by a great number of the most respectable ladies of Charleston—the first honor of the kind I ever experienced. Dined with the Members of the Cincinnati and in the evening went to a very elegant dancing Assembly at the Exchange, at which were 256 elegantly dressed & handsome ladies." The museum has an extraordinary collection of furniture made in

A view of the back facade of the Heyward-Washington House in the 1930s. Courtesy of the Library of Congress, HABS survey

Charleston, in addition to its other treasures, and the tour exits through the back door out into the formal garden, which is an approximation of what might have existed during the latter half of the 1700s.

In her book on eighteenth-century American gardens, Ann Leighton says of Charleston,

> Gardens had always been a prime consideration, but it is a rewarding and pleasurable confirmation to find that in the record books of property transfers of the eighteenth century, the "Plat Books" trace out garden

The same view of the garden more than eighty years later

The gate entrance in June. The small tree is a dogwood.

plans as well as boundaries and house sites. In almost every case the garden is shown to be laid out in a pattern of square or rectangular beds, with a central feature in a little circle and perhaps quarter circles in the corners. Sometimes an orchard or vegetable garden is included in an overall formal design.

Ann Leighton, *American Gardens in the Eighteenth Century "For Use or for Delight"*

THE NATHANIEL RUSSELL HOUSE

Built on lower Meeting Street in 1808 by a wealthy merchant, this handsome brick mansion with its monogrammed decorative ironwork became a house museum in the 1950s when it was purchased by Historic Charleston Foundation. There was always a beautiful and well-cared-for garden adjacent to the house, and this tradition has been maintained by the foundation.

Photographs and drawings from the early part of this century show a wooden fence in front of the house. The Pelzer family, who lived in the Russell House for almost fifty years before it became a museum, added the handsome brick and wrought-iron fence and gates, which were copies of ones surrounding a mansion that no longer exists on the corner of Meeting and George Streets. Francis Pelzer also planted the pair of mature *Magnolia grandiflora* trees and some of the maples that grace the garden today. Under the expert guidance of Robert Cox, the gardens are maintained by professionals as well as skilled volunteers. Many of the plants are labeled.

A garden chronology notes some highlights of the garden during its heyday: "An English visitor in 1819 praises the 'bowers of myrtles, oranges, and lemons, smothered with fruit and flowers' in his diary. Citrus trees still produce fruit in the garden today." In 1827 Mrs. Russell wrote to her grandson that "my family of Silk Worms (they dined on mulberry tree leaves) have all

The Nathaniel Russell House

completed their Work above a week ago, each one a beautiful ball of Silk from which they are now eating their way thro' as butterflys."

The garden was reworked and enriched from 1859 to 1861 by the Allston family. Mr. Allston hired a gardener and brought in a slave to help with the work. He ordered forty-eight loads of earth for the flower beds and multiple loads of shell for the paths.

The house was damaged by mortar shells during the Civil War. In 1870 it was sold to the Sisters of Charity of Our Lady of Mercy, who owned it for thirty-eight years. The Mullally family owned it next, and a granddaughter recalls that the garden was "divided into three sections with a formal, parterre

In the garden, looking toward Meeting Street

garden in the front, a grassy section for children to play in in the middle, and a work yard with a cow, a pony, and chickens in the rear."

During the time that the Pelzer family and their five children occupied the house, the book *Carolina Gardens* was written by E. T. H. Shaffer. He describes the garden in part: "Here the patterned beds of flowers are separated from the kitchen garden by a thick hedge of althaeas, giving beauty to both. Tall oleanders reach up to the monogram of the builder. From the gate the path is bordered with English box; just inside the gate, looking over the wall, are large crape myrtles. . . . The garden is lovely with pomegranates, with spikenard, the pale shadowy tamarisk, and everywhere the blue sky caught to earth in pools of blue larkspur" (courtesy of Historic Charleston Foundation).

After the foundation took over the house, its director, Frances Edmunds, who was also a gardener, took over the grounds with help from several other garden devotees. Archeological research was not conclusive enough to reproduce the 1808 garden, but Mrs. Edmunds consulted local and national designers and landscape architects for help. She corresponded with Peter Hatch at Monticello: "We are interested in an appropriate period design for the garden," she wrote in 1982, shortly before her retirement. She was instrumental in hiring Rudy Favretti to draw the design for the garden that for the most part exists today. Mr. Favretti supplied an extensive list of authentic plants for restoring and reproducing period landscapes that served as an inspiration and a starting point. Today Bob Cox works with plant material that is "tried and true" and keeps up with soil tests and maintaining good drainage and plant care.

Maples and palms are some of the trees planted along with live oaks on the main campus of the College of Charleston. The pastel colors of spring are replaced with red and cool white plantings in summer, shown here around the large fountain behind Randolph Hall.

Academic Gardens

It is no surprise that locations where learning takes place frequently have gardens. Many campuses nationwide are certified arboretums and have garden areas where students can enjoy beauty outdoors. The College of Charleston, founded in 1770, is the oldest educational institution south of Virginia and the nation's first municipal college. Today its beautiful buildings are surrounded by lovely plantings, many of which were chosen by Robert Marvin (1920–2001) of Walterboro, South Carolina. William P. Baldwin wrote that Mr. Marvin "was considered by many to be the South's most influential landscape architect."

Bougainvillea and elephant ears enhance a plaza and entrance to buildings on the Medical University of South Carolina campus.

To the right is a late spring view of a city street incorporated years ago into the main campus of the College of Charleston

A walk around the Medical University of South Carolina in Charleston shows that a tremendous effort has been made recently to introduce pretty combinations of plants that make the campus appealing. Both of the Trident Technical College locations show a similar effort. Julian Mitchell Math and Science Elementary School has a working vegetable garden, while the Charleston Parks Conservancy, which is not a school, has educational programs that take place in parks and gardens. The Horticultural Society has numerous educational workshops and lectures and works closely with volunteers to beautify the South Windermere neighborhood where it is located.

ASHLEY HALL

The address of Charleston's finest Regency villa is number 172 on Rutledge Avenue, a street noted for its nineteenth-century mansions. The imposing house faces south on approximately two acres enclosed by fences and brick walls. When it was built sometime around 1820, the bricks for its construction were formed and fired in a kiln that is now part of its solid foundation.

Only four families inhabited the villa before Miss Mary Vardrine McBee purchased it in 1909 from the estate of Charles Otto Witte for the girls' school she named Ashley Hall. The school has flourished and grown over the years, and the house, with its later additions, has been preserved and renovated.

Ashley Hall school's main building is a Regency villa on Rutledge Avenue. Boxwood hedges surround the pool and fountain at the entrance to the school.

The Witte family lived on the property from 1879 to 1908. Their garden legacy is eccentric and notable. Mr. Witte adored his wife and six daughters, and he loved gardening. He also had a wonderful sense of the "genius loci," made famous by the seventeenth-century poet Alexander Pope and later embraced by generations of landscape architects:

> Consult the genius of the place in all;
> That tells the waters or to rise, or fall;
> Or helps th' ambitious hill the heav'ns to scale,
> Or scoops in circling theatres the vale;
> Calls in the country, catches opening glades,

Joins willing woods, and varies shades from shades,
Now breaks, or now directs, th' intending lines;
Paints as you plant, and, as you work, designs.

An avid gardener, Mr. Witte created a landscape full of fragrant and colorful garden walks, with bowers of roses and masses of cutting flowers for the household. According to the historian Ileana Strauch, "when Comings Creek, above Calhoun Street, was stopped up, Witte filled in the marsh to the east and added it to his grounds."

He collected rare specimens and exotic plants that were kept in greenhouses and added a menagerie of imported animals. Near the house a grotto of phosphate rock was constructed, along with a fish pool. Across from the mansion, a garden folly was built to serve as an aviary.

One of Witte's daughters, Laura Witte Waring, wrote about growing up in Charleston and described her father's passion.

Shell House was originally built as an aviary for exotic birds. It is now a meeting place for seniors. The grotto is off to the left beyond the boxwood hedge.

> His hobby was his garden and the birds. Every day when dinner was over he left the table with some fruit, which he divided among the birds. All afternoon, unless he drove out with my mother, he spent working in the garden, supervising the planting and renewal of the soil, potting the cuttings and young plants, and putting new bulbs and seeds in the ground, so that the flower beds and the greenhouses were always kept to standard. At one point the entire grounds were filled with beautiful gardens and fantastic floral walkways.
>
> Here and there in the garden were benches, carved seats, an occasional iron table, a painted Indian warrior, a large iron deer, and various smaller bronze and iron animals, characteristic of Victorian gardens. If the iron figures, the many birdhouses, ponds and fountains, and garden furniture seem fantastic now, they were fashionable in their day, and now can be thought of with amusement. Nothing can mar the enchantment of a garden that has been a part of one's earliest life, and thereby retained in love and memory.
>
> Hiding the back part of the garden were cane, banana trees, strawberry and banana shrubs; plum trees which bore fruit in season, jujube and mulberry trees, and persimmon trees which bore orange-red persimmons in the autumn.
>
> Behind the garden were vegetable beds, laid out formally with paths between. Lettuce, carrots, radishes, parsley, asparagus and burr artichokes were planted.
>
> From *The Way It Was in Charleston as Recalled by Laura Witte Waring* (2010)

Mrs. Waring goes on to describe some of the animals the family loved and kept. There were horses, ponies, burros, dogs, cats, guinea pigs, turtles, goldfish, and "there was always a cow."

"Exit, pursued by a bear" (William Shakespeare, *The Winter's Tale*)—The grotto was nicknamed the "Bear Cave." School tradition includes the production of Shakespearean plays, and this quirky rock formation, with its several caves and its terrace, makes a perfect stage set in good weather. Another grotto around the corner has a pond with goldfish and turtles.

The family's best-known pet was a bear cub that was given to a zoological garden when it grew too large. Other pets included an alligator named Wishy-Washy, monkeys, prairie dogs, and even a family of opossums. Shell house, which served as the aviary, is covered in conch shells and has a glass roof. Cockatoos, macaws, parrots, parakeets, love birds and many other species of small birds inhabited the little house. Larger birds were also kept on the property: silver and golden pheasants; peacocks; ducks, turkeys, and chickens. A keeper was employed to manage all the animals, and there were various buildings that housed and protected them. An underground tank kept the prairie dogs from burrowing around the city.

When the property became a school, a library, auditorium, pool building, tennis courts, gymnasium, lower school, and more classroom buildings were gradually added as Ashley Hall grew in popularity. For many years there were boarding students, most of whom lived in McBee House; that house is now a day school.

Vestiges of past glory remain: there are several magnificent live oaks and a venerable cedar, but the formal flower gardens are gone. There are still lawns and benches and quiet places to sit and to gather, and the campus is a lovely place to visit. T. Hunter McEaddy, a local landscape architect, helped the school rebuild the pool and fountain near the Rutledge Avenue entrance. Here formal boxwood parterres were successfully planted, as Mr. McEaddy put it, in a "purposeful design that worked." Antique roses were planted along the eastern entrance, along with palmettos and hedges to break up and soften building facades. The infrastructure of terraces, drains, and paths was carefully addressed. Mr. McEaddy emphasized the importance of introducing large planters full of flowers, the point being to have background material that does not require heavy maintenance and provides seasonal color and a welcoming "show."

The student body has recently taken an interest in ecological gardening. A new rooftop garden on the science building was established in January 2013. Its purpose is to grow plants and succulents to "create a micro-climate that moderates the temperature above and below and assists with water retention." The area is also intended to be "an attractive environment for butterflies and birds and to provide a living laboratory for students." In the lower grades the little ones have a sweetly decorated and raked sandy patch in the shade alongside one of the buildings; this they call their Zen garden. There are efforts to create small community, medicinal, and native plant gardens as well. The house and the grounds are open to visitors by appointment.

THE GARDENS AT THE MEDICAL UNIVERSITY OF SOUTH CAROLINA

The well-labeled sunny raised beds of the medicinal garden show herbs and foxglove in bloom, and there are black fabric sails in the background beds to protect the shade-loving plants. Long, low walls and benches provide seating.

In June 2012 I read a newspaper account of vegetables being grown on the campus of the Medical University of South Carolina (MUSC), a sprawling mass of old and new buildings intersected by narrow streets located across the middle of the peninsula toward the Ashley River. The tenth-oldest medical school in the United States and the oldest in the Deep South, it was founded in 1824. I thought that I would go investigate when my interest was really piqued by news in May 2013 that the university had just received certification from the National Arboretum as a Tree Campus USA. I was delighted with my visit and have gone back again and again.

The idea behind the gardens and the arboretum is that patients seem to get better more quickly when they have access to the soothing beauty of a garden. To this end there is a healing garden in an atrium formed by the buildings of the Hollings Cancer Center. This lush, quiet oasis of semitropical plants has a central covered seating area and several seating pods off the winding walking path. Donated by Edwin and Barbara Pearlstine and designed by Robert Chesnut in 2008, it also features water falling gently from one pool into another. Although it is small and can be viewed all at once, it offers beauty, tranquility, and some privacy within the busy facility.

The arboretum has an educational variety of native and other trees. At last count there were more than 2,050 trees on campus, including the 'Shinseiki' and 'Tennosui' Asian pear; 'Granny Smith', Red Fuji, and 'White Winter Pearmain' apple; 'Giant Fuyu' persimmon; and Meyer lemon citrus trees planted near the medicinal garden.

The Urban Farm at the Medical University of South Carolina was once a parking lot used for large equipment.

Sabal palms, crape myrtles, and oaks make up most of the tree population, but the comprehensive list found on the arboretum website includes elm, holly, maple, pine, juniper, redbay, hornbeam, cedar, sycamore, bald cypress, willow, gingko, magnolia, hickory, ash, river birch, zelkova, cypress, camphor, cherry laurel, and arborvitae trees. Some of the blooming trees are cherry, 'Bradford' pear, crabapple, tea olive, dogwood, and redbud. The website not only lists the trees but also gives full descriptions and is thus a handy reference for identification. Native trees have their own list. To celebrate

National Arbor Day on April 26, 2013, one of the MUSC urban farm gardeners gave a lecture on attracting birds and wildlife to the garden, and outside experts gave short teaching sessions on how to maintain a backyard orchard, along with proper tree planting and establishment techniques.

The medicinal garden is located in a sheltered area close to the urban farm. It is an exhibition garden that includes many of the plants Dr. Francis Peyre Porcher wrote about in his 1863 book, *Resources of the Southern Fields and Forests*. Commissioned by the surgeon general of the Confederate States of America, this book was written "to identify substitutes for the manufactured drugs that were unavailable because of the Union blockade of southern ports and the lack of southern pharmaceutical laboratories."

The garden is well labeled with large signs telling about each plant and its uses during the time of the Civil War. There are herbs used in tonics, teas, and infusions made to treat nausea, fevers, constipation, hysteria, and syphilis.

MUSC URBAN FARM

Okra

Plant: Soak okra seeds in warm water for twenty-four hours before planting and keep the soil temperature at 24°C (75°F) or above. Soil should be fertile and high in potash. Transplant okra in a sunny location after last the frost. Space 1-2' apart in rows 2' apart. Row covers or plastic mulch will encourage early pod set. Okra is a tropical plant therefore requiring warm weather conditions.

Grow: Okra should be sown late in the spring or early summer when the ground is warm. Okra should then be thinned so the plants are spaced 12 to 18 inches apart. Keep moist and and fertilize well.

Harvest: Okra is a tall and attractive plant, okra grows very quickly and should be harvested frequently while it is still tender. Harvesting every few days will prevent toughness. For most tender and flavourful quality, harvest okra when pods are 3-4" long and cook as soon as possible. Pick okra on a weekly basis to encourage continual fruit set.

Nutritional Information:

Okra is fat free, cholesterol free, very low sodium, low calorie, an excellent source of vitamin C, and a good source of folate, magnesium and fiber.

How to Prepare: For best cooking results, okra should be fresh (not frozen). The pods should be small (3 inches or so long), or the okra becomes tough and stringy. If forced to use frozen okra, remove as much of the moisture as possible before cooking by spreading on a paper towel, or patting it dry after it thaws, etc. Okra is great vegetable in stews and gumbos.

Nutrition Facts

Serving Size 7 (3 inch) pods (83g)
Servings Per Container

Amount Per Serving	
Calories 25	Calories from Fat 0
	% Daily Value*
Total Fat 0g	0%
Saturated Fat 0g	0%
Trans Fat 0g	
Cholesterol 0mg	0%
Sodium 5mg	0%
Total Carbohydrate 6g	2%
Dietary Fiber 3g	12%
Sugars 1g	
Protein 2g	
Vitamin A 6%	• Vitamin C 30%
Calcium 6%	• Iron 4%

This sheet is an example of the information given out at the farm and on the website. Courtesy of the Medical University of South Carolina.

The leaves of some plants were used as poultices or as aromatic stimulants. The website for this garden shows the planting plan and notes the therapeutic uses of each plant. Many of the flowers are brightly colored and quite decorative, such as the Indian pink (*Spigelia marilandica*) and the yellow common tansy. Nearby, a butterfly garden is being established.

The Urban Farm at the medical university, located at the corner of Bee and President Streets, was a wonderful surprise. Several years ago the half-acre garden of rows and rows of vegetables, herbs, and bee-attracting flowers was an asphalt parking lot. I entered from the south, walking toward the School of Nursing. Beds full of 'Knockout' roses lead to the main entrance to the farm. A sign warning that there is an active bee hive is posted at the fence, but the organic vegetable patch is welcoming and hospitable. An oak tree shades a patio full of teak benches, and the rural-style shed beyond the tree houses tools and has facilities for cooking and other demonstrations.

In keeping with the concept that more green space was needed on the campus, the university had planned to plant the parking lot. It was their landscape architect, Bill Eubanks, who suggested a small garden to promote MUSC's commitment to health and wellness.

This is an educational garden, the brainchild of a dedicated group devoted to improving the lives of others, largely through learning about proper nutrition but also through the joys of gardening. There are school programs, lectures on various topics, tours, regular volunteer work and learn days, and community outreach initiatives. Those who attend the volunteer work days can take home produce in addition to a wealth of information on how to establish one's own vegetable garden. During the growing season there is a farmers' market at the "horseshoe" entrance on Rutledge Avenue. Vendors from the community are invited, too.

The farm has a comprehensive website that lists every plant in the garden and gives not only cultural and nutritional information but also recipes. I was impressed by the efficient design and layout of the raised beds, which incorporate flexible pipe as support for covers (if needed) and as frames for bird netting. I saw beds of different lettuces, tomatoes, eggplant, beans, corn, okra, squash, cucumbers, cabbage, culinary herbs, zinnias (to attract pollinators), and blueberries during one of my visits.

Dr. Susan Johnson is the enthusiastic director of the farm. She emphasizes that the project is a team effort to educate the community about healthy eating. The team is comprised of a grounds crew, dieticians, nutritionists, full-time gardeners, consultants, and volunteers. A food-distribution coordinator makes sure that organizations such as the Lowcountry Food Bank receive fresh produce. The medical university now hopes to help other hospitals and institutions start similar programs. Only a little more than a year old, the farm, she says, "has been successful beyond our wildest dreams."

Azaleas are in full bloom under live oaks
on the Battery.

CITY PARKS

The Charleston community has always had enthusiastic support for its parks. The first Board of Park Commissioners was created in 1895, when only White Point Garden, Washington Square, and Colonial Lake were owned by the city. Before 1760 there was a public garden along what is now Orange Street created for strolling and attending concerts near Broad Street. In the nineteenth century Charleston had its own small version of the famous English Vauxhall Gardens in an area bounded by King, Queen, and Broad Streets, and further uptown there was an ice cream parlor at the entrance to a garden with eleven pavilions.

A nineteenth-century park in Charleston had an outdoor ice cream parlor. Courtesy of the Charleston Museum

Today there are more than 120 parks and open spaces totaling 1,757 acres on the peninsula, Daniel Island, James Island, Johns Island, and west of the Ashley River. Hampton Park is the largest of the public parks, and the smallest is simply a pair of benches under an oak tree at the end of Murray Boulevard in front of the Coast Guard Station.

The range of recreational activities offered is a broad one and includes a superb volunteer program that allows participants to garden outdoors and in the greenhouses. New parks are always in the plans; two were completed downtown in May 2013: one at the eastern end of Charlotte Street and another in the triangle where Logan Street meets Beaufain Street. The Charleston Parks Conservancy is currently working on a planting plan for Colonial Lake, a popular spot for walking, jogging, fishing, and enjoying the tidewater pond that is overlooked by historic houses.

THE CHARLESTON PARKS CONSERVANCY

In 2007 the philanthropist Darla Moore founded the Charleston Parks Conservancy, an organization independent of the city that is dedicated to coordinating and educating a cadre of volunteers whose activities center around the city's parks. This dynamic group's program coordinator, the horticulturist Jim Martin, feels that the conservancy "is a reflection of the Charleston community as a whole and how that community relates to its public green spaces and to each other. The education of the community is of paramount importance. We work hard to make sure everyone benefits." The conservancy has a comprehensive website featuring information on plants, instructional videos, and information on the work sites, play sites, educational opportunities, and gatherings it sponsors. It works closely with the Horticultural Society, Historic Charleston Foundation, and the Preservation Society, and has recently worked with a graduate program at the College of Charleston. Renovation, reinvention, restoration, and maintenance, along with fundraising, are part of the conservancy's mission. So are community gardens.

Through projects and programs for all ages, and through caring for the land, the conservancy brings people together in many ways, often right in their own neighborhoods. A small plot can be leased annually in the community vegetable gardens, but some areas of the land are dedicated to providing produce donated to the Lowcountry Food Bank. When large trees have to be removed, a local artisan, David Avutek, asks permission to obtain some of the useful wood, and he turns it into artisan bowls that are sold at the Historic Charleston Foundation shops, with a percentage of the sales benefitting the Charleston Parks Conservancy. The conservancy is active in almost all of Charleston's parks, but Hampton Park is an exception.

HAMPTON PARK

In 2012 History Press published *A History of Charleston's Hampton Park* by Kevin R. Eberle, a resident of the neighborhood surrounding the park. His account is fascinating. The general area of the park is located at the top of the peninsula along the eastern bank of the Ashley River approximately three miles north of the Battery, and it was in use beginning in the early eighteenth century. Records show exports in 1737 of oranges, nectarines, bananas, pomegranates, olives, and figs grown on the farm there that was called Orange Grove Plantation. (The "Great Freeze" of 1747 ended most of the citrus production around Charleston.) A later map shows formal gardens and a greenhouse surrounding the plantation house before it was burned during the Revolutionary War when the British marched down the peninsula. In 1786 an English immigrant built another plantation house on the same land, in a different location. This building, now known as Lowndes Grove, stands today, although there have been many modifications over the years. In the late 1800s the property, consisting of about 250 acres, was acquired by Captain Frederick W. Wagener, a wealthy tradesman and entrepreneur. He was instrumental in organizing what would become the only world's fair ever held in South Carolina, and he lent his farm for that purpose.

The South Carolina Interstate and West Indian Exposition opened on December 1, 1901, with great fanfare. The city was rebuilding and recovering from the great earthquake of 1886, and cotton was the state's largest cash crop. President Theodore Roosevelt came to the exposition, arriving by steamboat. Thomas Edison made a film clip of the president, with the first

The Chapel Street Fountain Park is maintained by the Charleston Parks Conservancy. Mayor Joseph P. Riley Jr. donated the live oak in the background.

lady by his side, reviewing the army, navy, and marine corps foot soldiers in April 1902 on the steps of one of the columned buildings.

There were more than twelve monumental and elaborate buildings that were really just stage sets: temporary gems with plaster-type ornamentation all painted white, earning the exposition the nickname "The Ivory City." Just three of the buildings covered more than one hundred thousand square feet. The emphasis of the exhibits was more on agriculture and industrialism than on horticulture, although there was a Japanese garden recreated inside the Fair Japan Building. Two lakes made a figure-eight shape, part of which was the forty-acre Lake Juanita, formed by damming a cove of the Ashley River to the west. Sunken gardens lay to the east.

The sunken gardens at the South Carolina Interstate and West Indian Exposition 1901–1902. Courtesy of the Lowcountry Digital Library, College of Charleston

The Lowndes Grove house was used as the "Woman's Building." There was a forested garden walk featuring sculpture that was billed as "Lovers' Lane in the Garden of Eden," according to the official guidebook. Most of the sculpture was modeled in a mix of concrete, plaster, and jute that deteriorated quickly and fell apart within a few years. An early video shows visitors strolling the grounds, as well as a panoramic view of some of the main buildings. The video can be accessed through the Library of Congress.

There were few, if any, trees on the main exposition grounds. The midway alone took up thirty acres. There had been a famous racetrack on the property in the 1700s, and Captain Wagener maintained his own racetrack in the late 1800s. Much of the area had been used as a Confederate encampment during the Civil War and was later used for "warehousing" thousands of Union prisoners of war. On May 1, 1865, a parade of ten thousand marched at the site in honor of the prisoners on both sides who had died in the camps. This event became our country's first Memorial Day.

The South Carolina Interstate and West Indian Exposition was a financial failure and closed on May 31, 1902, after only six months and 675,000 visitors. Soon after, the City of Charleston purchased a section of the grounds and named it Hampton Park in honor of the Civil War hero General Wade Hampton, who had died the year the exposition closed.

The Court of Palaces, the Cotton Palace, and other buildings were torn down or collapsed; at least two of them burned. Vestiges of the sunken gardens lasted for more than ten years. The bandstand, although simplified and containing no original material, remains today.

Postcards of the gardens in the 1950s. Courtesy of JoAnn Breland

Mr. Eberle points out in his book on the park that the Clemson Agricultural Experiment Station was founded as a result of the exposition and that the Agricultural Society of South Carolina started plantings on the former fairgrounds as early as 1903. John Olmsted, the son and partner of Frederick Law Olmsted, the well-known landscape architect who designed Central Park in New York City, visited as a consultant for the new park.

In 1917 the park was again used as a military encampment, established on two of its acres. The military stable built at the time still remains; it was briefly the stable for the City of Charleston's horse patrol. In 1922 the city gave about two hundred acres of the western aspect of the park along the Ashley River to the Citadel, the Military College of South Carolina, which moved its campus there from its former location at Marion Square in the center of the peninsula.

During the first half of the twentieth century many visitors frequented the park, especially families coming on weekends to stroll among the

A rare aerial photograph of Hampton Park (heavily wooded area, center left) from the 1920s. Courtesy of the Citadel Archives and Museum

Helen Clark O'Brien (the author's mother-in-law) feeding the geese at Hampton Park

plantings and enjoy the outdoors. In early spring the huge azaleas along the one-mile drive around the main area of the park were a spectacular display of gaudy blooms. There was a concession stand selling Crackerjacks, candy, snacks, and soft drinks. Children loved to feed the ducks, geese, and other birds, but the park's largest attraction was its zoo. Newspaper accounts tell of an alligator pond and describe some of the zoo's inhabitants, many of which were given as gifts to the park. The list includes a buffalo, llamas, deer, prairie dogs, pheasants, a black swan, coyotes, goats, sheep, rabbits, raccoons, peacocks, a lion, a bear or two, six species of monkeys, and otters. There was also an aviary. Barry Bessinger wrote to the *City Paper* in February 2013: "My brother and I walked through Hampton Park every day to James Simmons Elementary School as kids back in the early to mid-1950s. I vividly remember the zoo with the monkeys, otters and the aviary houses and the bison. We would shake the cyclone fence enclosure of the bison to the point where he couldn't stand it anymore and he would snort and snort and charge the fence at us and actually just run into the fence trying to get at us. We would squeal like the scared school kids that we were and hightail it for home as fast as we could." The zoo eventually became run-down; it closed in 1975, and the park fell into disuse.

The Citadel made several offers to purchase a large section of the southwest corner of the park in order to build an outdoor amphitheater, an auditorium, and a school for graduate studies, but Mayor Joseph P. Riley Jr. vetoed these attempts, and Hampton Park remained intact. On the anniversary of his thirtieth year as mayor, a semicircular seating area with seven benches was installed in Riley's honor by the city's employees. It overlooks the fountain in the lagoon and is flanked by a pair of his favorite peppermint peach trees.

HORTICULTURE AT HAMPTON PARK

The Hampton Park lagoons today

Jan Franklin, a gardening visionary who was hired by the City of Charleston in 1976, had a major impact on the parks. She turned a trash-filled World War I Quonset hut at the northern end of Hampton Park into the city's first greenhouse and began propagating plants and starting seeds. Today, eleven to fifteen thousand tropicals, semitropicals, and other plants are propagated, and more than forty thousand annuals are grown from seed. Now on the property there are several greenhouses used for growing plants to be distributed throughout the city.

A major renovation of Hampton Park took place in 1983 and 1984. The lagoon was full of stagnant water, and its bridges were unsound. Landscape

A bright mix of perennials along the walk by the lagoon in June

architects were consulted, and a plan developed wide walks along the present-day perennial and annual beds that surround the small double lagoon and its fountain. Charleston Trees, a committee of the Charleston Horticultural Society, raised money to plant more trees in addition to the hundreds planted since the exposition.

The first rose hybridized in America (ca. 1811) was Champney's Pink Cluster, the first of the Noisette class of roses. In 2001 the International Rose Heritage Conference held its ninth meeting in Charleston, which featured these roses, and the collection was showcased at Hampton Park and in other areas of the city.

Today the 63.9 acres comprising Hampton Park are managed by a small staff, but the park has a loyal core of about fifty volunteers, out of a group of more than two hundred who sign up regularly. This large number of volunteers is in large part a result of the magnetism of JoAnn Breland, the park's horticulturist for more than twenty-eight years.

Mrs. Breland's enthusiasm is contagious. She is a self-described "plant nerd" who personally chooses most of the plant displays not only for Hampton Park but also for many of the other Charleston parks. She enjoys playing with hundreds of color and texture combinations and often changes groupings. According to Mrs. Breland, a plant may be taken out of the scheme one year and reappear a couple of years later, just to keep things interesting.

The fifteen flower beds at Hampton Park are a wonderful mixture of plants and seeds from the greenhouses, gifts from volunteers and friends, showy collections, and experiments. Laurence Walker, who was a director of Historic Charleston Foundation and a dedicated gardener, wanted the park to have a comprehensive collection of amaryllis bulbs. He propagated them and gave many to the park. Other gardeners have brought in unusual cuttings, such as the fig tree from Greece that thrives near the greenhouses. Mrs. Breland has kept up with the Noisette roses, tried a hydrangea shade-walk (a failure due to a lack of water pressure), and started colorful collec-

A corner garden in a neighborhood bordering Hampton Park features colorful crotons and salvias. The half-moon bed of clipped Asiatic jasmine mirrors the arches of the house.

tions of *Aquilegia* (columbine) and *Acalypha* (copper plant). There are gaudy native gladioli, African foxgloves, and mounds of *Convolvulus tricolor* (dwarf morning glory bush), as well as the much-loved and familiar zinnias, calendulas, pansies, and snapdragons. Volunteers help propagate cuttings, start seeds, and assist in planting the beds. Specialists take care of the turf, but staff members also plant and do all of the maintenance.

The park is rimmed with large old azaleas under oaks. There are magnolias and other shade trees over picnic tables. Runners and walkers can enjoy an obstacle course as well as flowerbeds bursting with color. The most

The Battery bandstand

important aspect of the park, though, says Mrs. Breland, is its availability to everyone. Marriages, family reunions, picnics, and a variety of other events take place on its grounds. "It is truly the people's park," she says proudly.

Sharing is a big part of her job. Garden clubs, school groups, and others can schedule tours of the production and greenhouses. There is even an annual plant exchange. Regular volunteers can choose plants from the "market" she maintains for them. Mrs. Breland notes that she loves the new and the unusual, but the various showy and brilliant coleus plants are some of her very favorites. There are scads of variations in the greenhouse. Begonias are another of Mrs. Breland's pet plants, but it is a sweet white *Calamintha nepeta* (catnip) that was officially named for her.

THE BATTERY

The site of Fort Broughton in 1735, Fort Wilkins in 1812, and an artillery battery during the Civil War bombardment of the city in the 1860s, White Point Garden is part of a promenade around the southernmost edge of the peninsula overlooking the harbor at the junction of the Cooper and Ashley Rivers. Locals call it the Battery. Today the park is a simple grid of crushed oyster-shell walks through several dozen live oak trees and palmettos, with lawn and azaleas beneath the trees. In 1837 it became a public park. There was a public bathing house on the Ashley River side that was demolished in 1883. The sea wall, which had been completed in 1820, was ruined by a hurricane in 1893, but it was rebuilt and has withstood storms ever since. In 1907 the bandstand was erected as a gift to the city. For some twenty years Sunday evening concerts were played under its green tiled roof.

The story of the statues, monuments, cannons, guns, and other memorials and souvenirs that have been placed in the park over the years is well documented and told in detail by the author, historian, and Charlestonian Warren Ripley. In his booklet *The Battery: Charleston, South Carolina* (1977) he gives the history of each piece and its importance to the city and its people. He tells of the hanging of famous pirates from gallows erected on the point in 1718 and relates the sad story of the Hobson memorial with its surrounding paving of the states and names of the men who died in a collision of two American ships during maneuvers off the Azores. Mr. Ripley recounts the history of the early submarine *H. L. Hunley*, which was pulled out of the Charleston harbor several years ago with its tragic contents, including the bones of the crew. There are monumental statues and pyramids of cannon balls, as well as large and small cannons and guns placed throughout the park. The local sculptor Willard Hirsch fashioned a charming statue and fountain for children. I remember going to the park as a child to talk to a man named Mr. Wagner and pat his horses. He was the first in my generation to give carriage rides, and he always parked at the Battery. My friends and I often exercised our dogs there and hunted for small shark's teeth in the gritty mix of sand and shell on the paths.

One of Mr. Ripley's most fascinating accounts is the story of the Keokuk gun, which he asserts is Charleston's most historic cannon, as it "served both sides during the Civil War and was the subject of a daring salvage operation." He goes on to tell how, after the Union ship *Keokuk*, an experimental iron-clad carrying a pair of eleven-inch Dahlgren guns, sank in shallow water in the harbor off of Morris Island, Confederate soldiers snuck aboard to try to salvage the huge guns.

> Night after night, these men braved death and hardship, working without lights, in absolute silence. Sound carries well at night and they were less than a mile from the enemy.
>
> With crowbar and wrench they began ripping open the heavy iron turrets. . . . [They managed to open] the turrets, but the Dahlgrens

The Battery in the late nineteenth century. The gun from the Union ship *Keokuk* can be seen in the foreground. Courtesy of the Library of Congress

The Fort Sumter Confederate monument overlooks the harbor and the fort a few miles to the east. Oleanders, planted all along the boulevard and against the sea wall, bloom in the heat of summer.

> remained inside, locked to their carriages by heavily bolted capsquares over the trunnions.
>
> A man, weighted by a heavy wrench, then took a breath and dropped into the chasm of blackness inside each turret. Feeling his way, he would find a capsquare, fit the wrench to the nut holding it, and try to push it a turn or two. Then up again, lungs crying for air, to bob gasping amid the waves breaking over the turret edge while a companion took his place at the wrench below.

The tale goes on to recount towing out one of the guns at night when the tide and weather were favorable. The workers were guarded by two Confederate ironclads and managed to steal away with their prize under harrowing circumstances. The retrieval of the second gun went more smoothly.

> The entire operation had taken roughly two and a half weeks and gave Charleston two excellent weapons, the largest in the South at that period. . . .
>
> One of the Dahlgrens was used at Fort Sumter and later returned to the city where it was mounted on The Battery, less than 50 feet from its mate today. It disappeared after the war and was likely sold as scrap.
>
> The weapon here today initially was sent to Battery Bee on Sullivan's Island where it was [used] against the original owners. . . .
>
> Abandoned at the evacuation of Charleston in February, 1865, it eventually fell from its rotting carriage and was covered by drifting sand. Near the turn of the century, it was discovered, authenticated, and sent to the city where in August, 1899, it was mounted in the park.

In addition to the permanent pieces on the Battery, temporary sculptures of natural and unusual materials have been on view from time to time at the park during the annual Spoleto Festival USA in May and June. On June 28, 2007, Carolina Day, a new memorial was dedicated. It is a bronze statue of Revolutionary War hero General William Moultrie by Charleston sculptor Jon Michel, who also made the statue of George Washington in Washington Square.

The Battery has always been a favorite place for residents and visitors to enjoy views of the harbor, Fort Sumter, the surrounding islands, and the elegant architecture of the area. And, in a sense, it has become a garden of remembrance.

> I'll trace these gardens o'er and o'er,
> Meditate on each sweet flower,
> Thinking of each happy hour,
> Oh, Johnny has gone for a soldier.
>
> *Traditional lament*

CANNON PARK

Situated directly across from Roper St. Francis Hospital is a small park of almost three acres of filled land that was given to the city in the early 1800s. A convention hall that could seat seven thousand visitors was designed by the North Carolina architect Frank P. Milburn and finished in 1899. Plans for the landscape were drawn by the Olmsted firm but never implemented. Infrequently used, the building became a theater, a hospital, and the site of the Charleston Museum, until it burned in 1981. Only the columns and steps, which have been stabilized and preserved, remain.

The columns of the old Charleston Museum are a dramatic backdrop for roses and crinum lilies.

One unusual feature in the park is an artesian well that is still used today. By definition, it is a well of water that rises naturally under pressure from a permeable stratum overlaid by impermeable rock. Many Charleston residents carry the water home for drinking and for cooking.

The park is well used today by locals, as there is no leash law for dogs. There is a small playground, and there are plenty of benches under the shade of mature oak trees. The Charleston Parks Conservancy has planted roses, crinum lilies, succulents, vines, and colorful perennials on the site.

JOSEPH P. RILEY JR. PARK

The former Waterfront Park, a longtime favorite of former Charleston mayor Joseph P. Riley Jr. was renamed in his honor. He feels that this public area, in particular, is a natural part of the fabric of the city. In 1978 Stu Dawson, a principal founder of the international landscape architectural firm Sasaki, was consulted to transform approximately eight acres along the waterfront from surface parking lots, vacant buildings, and ruined docks into a lovely park overlooking the Cooper River and the harbor.

Mayor Riley wanted to be certain that the consultants got it right. Instead of meeting the group on the site, he walked them all throughout the

Aerial view of Joseph P. Riley Jr. Park. Photograph courtesy of Sasaki Associates

historic district on the Lower Peninsula, down the alleys, and along the streets fronting the water on what Stu Dawson later referred to as a "forced march." When they finally arrived at their destination, they had a much better feel for the scale, the history, and the texture of the old city.

The park and a pair of multistory parking garages were not completed until 1990. The new park withstood the force of Hurricane Hugo in 1989 and has flourished since, winning numerous design awards. Today one can walk the 1,200-foot promenade along the marsh, sit on a swing, or watch people fishing on the pier. You can play Frisbee on a grassy lawn, have lunch on a sunny bench or at a picnic table under a roof on the dock, read in one of the

The area that subsequently became Waterfront Park. Photograph courtesy of Sasaki Associates

A view of the park and its water-jet and pineapple fountains on an early summer morning. The pineapple is a traditional symbol of hospitality.

shady garden rooms under the live oak trees, walk the dog, or splash with the children in the water jets of a fountain made for child's play. There is a wide sunny flower bed near this favorite water feature that has an ever-changing display of annuals and perennials. To top it off, the new City Art Gallery is right in the middle of the park.

MARION SQUARE

On a rainy May morning Danny Burbage, urban forester for the City of Charleston, gave me a tour of Marion Square. This former parade ground for the Citadel is jointly owned by the Washington Light Infantry and the

Sumter Guards. The city leases it, but with the stipulation that an open parade space always be maintained.

In 1750 a tabby fort was constructed on the property and served as a defense in the 1780 siege of Charleston. It was later named after Revolutionary war hero Francis Marion, also known as the Swamp Fox. The square is surrounded by main thoroughfares and wide sidewalks on three sides with the old Citadel taking up the northern boundary. Centrally located on the peninsula and comprising about six-and-one-half acres, it hosts a farmers' market from April through December and an artists' market during the Spoleto Festival USA. Other major events take place on the square during holidays, as well as during Fashion Week, the Food and Wine Festival, and

Visitors enjoying the farmers' market at Marion Square on a sunny day

the Southeastern Wildlife Exposition. It is also the unofficial "beach" for the College of Charleston's sun-loving students.

But the square has plenty of shade and benches and flowerbeds along its perimeters and is punctuated by significant monuments and two fountains, one old and one new. A haunting Holocaust Memorial commissioned by the City of Charleston and the Jewish Federation is centered along the Calhoun Street side, next to the eighty-foot column supporting a statue of the statesman John C. Calhoun. There is also a statue of General Wade Hampton that was relocated from Hampton Park when that park went into a decline.

The trees surrounding the open center of the park are diverse. A copse of single-trunk crape myrtles is centered along the western King Street

A statue of the statesman John C. Calhoun towers above garden beds and a variety of trees in Marion Square.

Palmetto debris on a city street

boundary. There are swamp white oaks (*Quercus bicolor*), live oaks, red oaks, laurel oaks, palmettos, Canary palms, fast-growing Kentucky coffee trees (*Gymnocladus dioica*), Chinese elms, and cherry trees. One also finds redbuds, a tulip poplar, and a trio of star magnolias. One of the largest sweet gum trees in the city lives on the square.

According to Mr. Burbage, the honey locusts that were given a try as street trees were failures, and the American elm will soon be reintroduced. As the elms succumbed to the ravages of Dutch elm disease, they were often replaced throughout the city with sturdy live oaks and palmettos. Trees throughout the city are diverse, and the urban forestry department continues to introduce as many successful new species as possible. A recent tree-frequency report of more than 17,000 trees shows 149 distinct species. Of these, 24 percent are live oaks, 19 percent are sabal palmettos, and 17 percent are crape myrtles. Mr. Burbage's favorite tree is the Angel Oak, now protected in a city park on Johns Island. This magnificent old survivor is said to be more than 500 years old.

Pruning trees is a major task for the city's staff, and there are frequent encounters with wildlife. "Whenever our arborists come across young birds or mammals, they leave them alone unless they pose a hazard. If they do have to be removed, they are sent to an appropriate place to be nurtured," explains

Mr. Burbage. Rats are an exception. "Rats are particularly fond of nesting high up in the palmettos, and our guys loathe it when the rodents jump into the buckets of the cherry pickers used to reach the dead palmetto fronds."

There are possums, raccoons, squirrels, and a wide variety of snakes, mostly nonpoisonous, that inhabit the trees. The entire city is a bird sanctuary with hundreds of species that can be watched throughout the year or when they are migrating. Our family had a woodcock in our walled garden after a particularly cold winter one year. Hawks have roosted on the weathervane of St. John's Lutheran Church for decades, and a pair of these raptors can often be seen hunting at Waterfront Park. I once witnessed a disoriented deer swimming across Colonial Lake.

COURTENAY SQUARE

On May 28, 2013, Mayor Joseph P. Riley Jr. and City of Charleston Fire chief Karen Brack dedicated a new park in the center of the Historic District. The site was originally intended as a park to honor Mayor William A. Courtenay, who, along with the Charleston City Council, established the first paid fire department in the city in 1882.

A small cast-iron pavilion was constructed on the lot in 1885. Then the great earthquake of 1886 caught the entire area by surprise, caused death and

The pavilion at the corner of Meeting and Wentworth Streets. The corner area is now a city park called Courtenay Square.

great destruction, and resulted in years of recovery. As a result of the earthquake many fires destroyed lives and buildings. Mayor Courtenay advocated building several centrally located fire stations, and construction on the one at the corner of Meeting and Wentworth Streets was begun that same year. The park was abandoned, but the pretty pavilion was left in situ, and the garages of the new fire station were built around it.

According to the *Charleston Post and Courier*, the site had been covered with concrete for more than a century. The city removed the concrete, restored the pavilion, and created planting beds overflowing with roses and flowering woody shrubs. Benches were added, and now the new park is a welcoming spot for visitors and residents. They can enjoy sun or shade in the midst of a busy retail district near restaurants and historic sites.

In the background is a Confederate monument. The bust in the foreground is of Henry Timrod, poet laureate of the Confederacy.

WASHINGTON SQUARE

When my husband and I were in the first years of our marriage, we bought a little house on Chalmers Street facing Washington Square. I would walk through the small park on my way to work on Broad Street, the next thoroughfare to the south. When our son was born, I often took him for a spin around the park in his pram or stroller. I loved the miniature granite copy of the Washington Monument in the center that was always surrounded by a colorful mix of annuals and perennials. The obelisk was erected by the Washington Light Infantry in 1881 as a memorial to the four hundred men of the infantry who died during the Civil War. One of its plaintive inscriptions reads:

> And she speaks in a voice that is sad as death,
> There is duty still to be done.
> Tho' the trumpet of onset has spent its breath,
> And the battle been lost and won.

The park was opened to the public in 1818 when the 1801 building that is now City Hall was conveyed to the city. City Hall sits on the southwest corner, Robert Mills's "Fireproof Building" that houses the South Carolina Historical Society is on the northwest corner, and the eastern boundary is a handsome brick wall. The roughly one-acre space is enclosed by a brick and wrought-iron fence, with three stunning wrought-iron gates giving entry from Broad, Meeting, and Chalmers Streets. Chalmers Street is particularly appealing because it is still cobbled. Wide brick walks traverse the park in the form of a cross with the forty-two-foot-high monument in the center. Live oaks and azaleas punctuate the corners and edges, and there are plenty of benches all around.

Very early in Charleston's history, the square was the site of a tavern. It was not fenced or gated in the late 1800s and served as a temporary tent city after the earthquake of 1886. For many years there was a famous statue of William Pitt facing Meeting Street to the west that has been removed to the Charleston Museum for the sake of its preservation. It has been replaced with a modern bronze statue of George Washington by the local sculptor Jon Michel. Other tributes include a statue of Henry Timrod and a monument to General P. G. T. Beauregard. The colorful flower mixes at the base of the central obelisk that remain today are seasonally replenished and serve to draw one toward the poetry on the monument.

DANIEL ISLAND

Originally inhabited by indigenous people and later granted to Robert Daniell, who became a governor of the Colony of Carolina, this four-thousand-acre island has been carefully and responsibly developed over the past sixteen years into an award-winning model community.

There are more than twenty parks and green spaces totaling four hundred acres on this island inhabited by approximately ten thousand citizens. According to the developers' statement, most of the parks are maintained by a property-owners association, but the City of Charleston has seven separate areas on the island that are maintained by the city and volunteers from the Charleston Parks Conservancy. Many amenities are offered, including a charming wading pool for children in the shape of Charleston Harbor and the Ashley and Cooper Rivers that extend along the peninsula. In addition to the parks there is a nature preserve riverwalk along the Wando River.

The Charleston Horticultural Society featured Daniel Island on its thirteenth annual fall tour known as Gardens for Gardeners. Because none of the gardens or parks is more than twenty years old, there is a wide variety of newer plant material, including the latest introductions available at local

The children's wading pool on Daniel Island is in the shape of Charleston Harbor. The peninsula is on the right.

plant nurseries. Exotic gingers, evergreen wisteria (*Millettia reticulata*), succulents, ornamental grasses, and the red-, green-, and white-striped tender perennial *Stromanthe* flourish in the gardens. One of the more unusual sights is fall color in the form of the Encore azalea, which blooms in spring and again in October, especially under the shade of the oak trees. Natural habitats have also been preserved in the parks and even in the private gardens. One pair of gardeners has obtained certification as a National Wildlife Federation Wildlife Habitat. On their property the numerous colorful plantings that attract butterflies, the bird and squirrel feeders, and the birdbaths all give evidence supporting this national designation.

Salvia, grasses, and palms along a road on Daniel Island

Starting in the late 1980s and continuing today, there has been a tremendous nationwide effort to make cities more livable. Mayor Joseph P. Riley Jr., the city's employees, the Parks Commission, the Charleston Garden Conservancy, the Charleston Horticultural Society, volunteers, neighborhood groups, garden clubs, preservation and numerous civic groups have worked together to make the parks in and around the city available to all, full of a variety of trees and plants, artistic, interesting, beautiful, educational, recreational, fun, and just plain good for the whole community. New parks are added at every opportunity. Each of them is a joy to view and to visit.

In the background, the Fort Moultrie Monument commemorates the June 28, 1777 Patriot victory over the British Fleet. This battle, the first decisive victory in the war for independence, is still celebrated annually as Carolina Day.

LIVE OAKS IN THE CITY

Icon through the ages, ancient symbol of strength and power endowed with mysterious properties, and infinitely useful, the oak tree is known to all through literature, poetry, song, sight, and familiar use. Here in the lowcountry we are fortunate to have public access to two of the grandest living trees in America, both of them live oaks (*Quercus Virginiana*). The Middleton Oak reaches over the edge of the Ashley River on the grounds of Middleton Place, about a thirty-minute drive north of Charleston. South of the city, also about thirty minutes from downtown, on Johns Island, the Angel Oak can be seen

This resilient old oak at Magnolia Cemetery is a survivor of Hurricane Hugo (1989).

in a small park created to protect this ancient survivor. Conflicting reports abound about which tree is the oldest, but the trees are similar in girth: the Middleton Oak was mapped in 2004 and had a girth of thirty-one feet, while the circumference of the Angel Oak measured about twenty-eight feet, also in 2004. Both may be well over one thousand years old, and both are on the National Register of Big Trees. A stand of 249 live oaks in City Park, New Orleans, is the largest group registered with the Live Oak Society, founded in 1934. Charleston's own live oak park, White Point Garden, became a public garden in 1837.

The live oak is a garden system unto itself. At about the age of one hundred, it typically produces more than one thousand acorns a year, providing a significant food source for white-tailed deer, black bears, wild pigs and turkeys, raccoons, squirrels, and rodents. Quail, wood ducks, jays, and yellow-bellied sapsuckers also rely on the annual crop. The yellow-crowned night-heron favors building nests in the live oaks in Charleston's Washington Park and can often be found roosting in the oaks on nearby Church Street. Bats roost in the live oaks, too.

Quercus Virginiana is the larval host for the hairstreak butterfly and the oakworm moth, as well as for several epiphytes. The most beloved of these is *Tillandsia usneoides*, or Spanish moss, a graceful gray ghost of trailing tendrils with tiny fragrant chartreuse blossoms. Ball moss (*Tillandsia recurvata*) also favors the oak. The abundant mistletoe, often mistaken for an epiphyte, is actually a parasite. Its green balls are camouflaged by the evergreen leaves of the live oak but are easily silhouetted against the bare winter branches of deciduous oaks and other host trees.

Numerous ferns take root on and around live oaks. One of the most interesting is the resurrection fern (*Polypodium polypodioides*), an epiphytic fern that seems to disappear in dry weather. After a good rain, it reappears in full glory up and down the branches. Lichens and mosses, mushrooms and fungi, bark, and leaf litter provide shelter and food for lizards, beetles, spiders, worms, cockroaches, and other insects. Snakes are frequently found in the vicinity looking for prey.

The live oak never completely loses all its leaves, shedding constantly, although largely in the spring. The leaves are tough and somewhat acidic. They break down slowly and make excellent mulch for azaleas and camellias. The male trees produce small yellowish-brown flower clusters called catkins; the female flowers are also usually clustered but can be single. Galls, not often harmful to the tree, are usually produced by various gall wasps. A young oak can grow more than two feet per year, and a mature oak can draw up to fifty gallons of water a day.

Settlers and colonists relied upon the oak, found along the coast from Virginia to Florida, for its strong, dense wood, the heaviest of all the American natives. An air-dried cubic foot weighs about fifty-five pounds. The English sought oaks for building ships for the Royal Navy. The twenty-five-inch-thick frame of Old Ironsides (the USS *Constitution*) was rebuilt with live oak sandwiched between white-oak planking. Live oaks had to be harvested from southern forests, and in 1828 President John Quincy Adams authorized the purchase of land near Pensacola, Florida, that became the first Naval Live Oaks Preserve.

The tree is so revered that it has become an icon of the South. After Hurricane Hugo in 1989 one Charlestonian donated enough funds for arborists to clean up and repair damage to the beloved oaks of White Point Garden.

CEMETERIES, CHURCHYARDS, AND GRAVEYARDS

THERE ARE MORE THAN twenty-five cemeteries on the Charleston peninsula alone. The earliest congregations in the city were established in the 1600s, starting with the Anglican church (now St. Philip's) and the Circular Congregational Church in 1681 and the First Baptist Church in 1682. St. Michael's Church, on the corner of Meeting and Broad Streets, is the oldest surviving church building in the city, dating from 1752, followed by the Unitarian Church, on which construction began in 1772.

By the early 1800s there was a shift toward suburban cemeteries, not only on account of lack of space and health concerns but also as a result of nineteenth-century idealism. In his introduction to *City of the Silent*, Ted Ashton Phillips Jr.'s book on Magnolia Cemetery, Thomas J. Brown writes: "The so-called rural cemetery movement reflected shifting religious and cultural ideas about death. The new institutions aimed to replace bleak and ominous church graveyards with sylvan spaces in which beautifully regenerating trees and flowers surrounded decorous memorials. The carefully wrought landscapes aspired to facilitate serene contemplation of the blissfully reposing dead and provide assurances of eternal life."

Thomas S. Klatka, a preservation officer with the Virginia Department of Historic Resources, writes that "the rural cemeteries were also known as 'garden' cemeteries due to the planned landscapes and lavish plantings that rivaled contemporary arboretums. Detailed design plans were followed to create 'natural' landscapes with ponds, curvilinear paths, and open spaces structured by rolling terrain and accentuated by carefully designed plantings of trees, shrubs, and flowers. Situated within these pastoral landscapes was the ornate, yet massive and imposing, architecture for the dead." Magnolia Cemetery, located at the city limits on the northeast side of the peninsula, is just such a place, with old moss-draped oaks and cedar trees, azaleas, and old-fashioned blooming shrubs and flowers.

FACING Unitarian Churchyard

MAGNOLIA CEMETERY

The groves were God's first temple.

William Cullen Bryant, 1794–1878

Magnolia Cemetery, dedicated in 1850 and Charleston's oldest public cemetery, has a glorious history that is beautifully told in Ted Ashton Phillips Jr.'s illustrated book, *City of the Silent: The Charlestonians of Magnolia Cemetery.* Situated on the northeastern aspect of the peninsula, just within the city boundaries, the old burial grounds are a tranquil garden of fascinating monuments surrounded by oaks, magnolias, hollies, palmettos, sago palms, cedars, and yuccas. In spring there are azaleas and roses and narcissus, followed by more roses and lilies in summer, then camellias and sasanquas in the fall. A picturesque wooden bridge crosses a small lake that draws egrets and other birds and wildlife. A recent visitor wrote on a travel website that she "loved the Spanish moss blowing in the wind."

It was not always so peaceful. In his introduction to Mr. Phillips's book, the editor Thomas J. Brown writes that during the Civil War "Confederate troops camped in the cemetery for three years and built breastworks in it for the defense of Charleston." He goes on to tell that "the famous 54th Massachusetts regiment camped at Magnolia after the occupation of Charleston in February 1864, and Union commanders allowed the troops to cut down for firewood a grove of oak trees that had been a centerpiece of the landscape design."

Today Magnolia is not only a place of memory for families and friends; it is also, and has always been, a tourist attraction and was touted as such in the advertisements around the time of the 1902 exposition. More than 2,200 Civil War veterans are buried behind its walls, including the last crew of the early submarine, the *H. L. Hunley*, which sank in Charleston Harbor and was recovered in 2000. In a recent abstract by Alfred L. Brophy titled "These Great and Beautiful Republics of the Dead," the author remarks on the beauty and order that rural cemeteries brought to the landscape; he further submits that they "served to mediate an impersonal, commercial world and brought uplift through the lessons of morality and patriotism that people learned when they visited." Originally landscaped in 1850 by Edward C. Jones, who would become a well-known Charleston architect, the grounds still retain vestiges of a grand plan.

We used to visit as children; it was one of many routine Sunday afternoon outings. My sister and I would explore while my family placed or planted flowers by the graves or pulled weeds and told us a little about our ancestors. My parents, paternal grandparents, maternal great-grandparents, and a good many other relatives and friends are buried in Magnolia Cemetery, and my mother gave me my first driving lesson on the dirt roads that wind throughout its 128 acres.

In a February 2013 interview published in the *Charleston Post and Courier*, Beverly Donald, superintendent of the cemetery for more than thirty years, called it the best-kept secret in Charleston. "This used to be a place of picnics," she remembers. "The trolley car came to the head of Cunnington Avenue. Visitors and lot owners would spend Saturdays picnicking and cleaning their lots. Now, you don't see as much of that, though it is starting to pick up more. Since the *Hunley* crew was buried here (in 2004), that's brought a lot

White camellias in full bloom in December

of people into the cemetery. I would venture to say we have close to 10,000 people a year."

Magnolia's offices are open daily during the week, and the gates are open from 8:00 A.M. until 6:00 P.M. every day.

THE UNITARIAN CHURCHYARD

Local records of original cemetery and churchyard plant material are scarce, but there are many treasures to be found in the landscapes of these sacred places. The Unitarian churchyard on Archdale Street is situated at the

A springtime view of the Unitarian and Lutheran church steeples from the Unitarian churchyard

In October swamp daisies bloom in profusion beneath the tower of the Unitarian Church.

western end of Gateway Walk, a pathway maintained by the Garden Club of Charleston. A brochure describes the walk as "designed to carry visitors through four of Charleston's oldest churchyards, past ornate monuments, wrought-iron gates, decorative fences, flowering plants, and ancient live-oak trees." The four churchyards belong to or belonged to at one time the Unitarian, Lutheran, Episcopal, and Congregational churches. Monuments in the Circular Congregational churchyard are the oldest and date back to the late 1600s.

A few months before Hurricane Hugo ravaged Charleston in 1989 the Unitarian Church hired Hugh and Mary Palmer Dargan of the landscape firm Dargan and Associates to survey and compile a grounds analysis of the old graveyard. Part of the analysis is a fascinating list of trees, shrubs, bulbs, flowers, vines, ferns, and weeds, complete with the dates of each plant's approximate discovery or introduction. There were seventeen species of trees, including *Tilia*, the linden or basswood that is called lime tree in Great Britain, and *Ailanthus altissima*, or tree-of-heaven that is a fast-growing and prolific seeder considered an ecological threat to native species. The iconic cedar grows in the graveyard, but there are no weeping willows.

Of the fifteen shrubs on the list, the Dargans noted that "all are introduced specimens with broad distribution and long association within this region. Roses are traditionally associated with memorials. Spiraea is a shrub planted for spring color . . . with several species represented but not yet identified. Aspidistra and nandina are frequently found in floral bouquets.

Gladioli, blue spiderwort, and a crinum lily bloom together in the Unitarian Churchyard.

Hydrangea is often planted on Mother's Day when it is available from florists. Althea 'Rose of Sharon' is a legacy plant and planted for its perpetual flowers in the summer. Breath-of-Spring is one of the first shrubs to bloom in the late winter. Cleyera and banana shrub (*Michelia figo*) are frequently cut for decorating. Banana shrub is significant for its infrequency; it is seldom found in local nurseries. Sasanqua camellia blooms when little else does at the beginning of winter." The Dargans go on to state that the choices of plant material in the cemetery are excellent for year-round color and that some of the plants may be rare varieties. There are colorful weeds spilling over the ground in somewhat controlled profusion: four o'clocks; morning glories;

Gladiolus byzantinus (1629) is an early spring bloomer in the Unitarian Church graveyard. Parts of the plant are poisonous, however, and handling it may cause allergies or skin irritation.

scarlet Turk's cap; and spiderwort. Ferns and ground covers vie with vines and bulbs for space. The enormous crinum lilies are spectacular when their trumpetlike flowers bloom in the summer and fall. Birds and other city wildlife make this urban sanctuary their home.

John Meffert, a devoted member of the Unitarian Church, works often with a group of volunteers who help maintain the churchyard. He calls the overflowing exuberance of the plant material "organized chaos" and emphasizes that Caroline Howard Gilman (1794–1888), a well-known writer and wife of longtime minister Samuel Gilman, was instrumental in shaping the way the graveyard is kept. She grew up near Boston's Mount Auburn cemetery, the prototype for the evocative rural landscaped burial ground founded by the Massachusetts Horticultural Society, and she wanted the churchyard in Charleston to be a place of beauty. She is buried with her husband in the Unitarian Churchyard beneath an elaborate memorial, in one of the city's prettiest and most romantic public gardens, where something is always in bloom.

15

STREET SCENES

A lovely planter by the street door of a single-house mansion

FACING A rack planter and window box lined with cocoa mat spill geraniums and annuals at the top of the entrance stairs to a grand house on Meeting Street.

Entry into the private gardens in the Historic District can often be achieved only during the annual fall and spring tours benefitting the Preservation Society and Historic Charleston Foundation. Even then, a limited number of tickets is sold. Happily, however, a surprising number of beautiful gardens can be seen from the street, often through handsome old wrought-iron gates and fences or from driveways. On some streets, such as Tradd, Meeting, and Queen, there seems to be a contest among neighbors to see who can come up with the prettiest and most unusual window box displays. Gardening is a passionate pursuit of many owners of historic properties, and it is a practice that has frequently been handed down through the generations. The well-known Charleston landscape architect Loutrel Briggs felt strongly that the garden was merely an extension of the house itself, and he designed accordingly. Charlestonians love to entertain and use their gardens frequently as outdoor rooms.

Walking the Lower Peninsula will give any gardener a solid foundation about what plants work best in each exposure on the compass, as well as an idea of the successful use of scale, repetition, texture, color, arrangement, direction, and form in the gardens that so beautifully complement the houses

The colors of these window-box plantings are spectacular against a Meeting Street house.

in the oldest sections of the city. We are fortunate that so many properties have brick and masonry walls that retain heat and can provide microclimates enabling the survival of many tender plants. The walls also provide privacy and places for wall fountains, sculptures, and espaliers.

Inscription for a Garden Wall:

Atmosphere

Winds blow the open grassy places bleak;
But where this old wall burns a sunny cheek,

They eddy over it too toppling weak
To blow the earth or anything self-clear;
Moisture and color and odor thicken here.
The hours of daylight gather atmosphere.
Robert Frost

In addition to learning about the plants that work well in Charleston gardens, the keen gardener can observe variation upon variation of paving patterns, wall construction, gates, fences, and decorations. There are many interesting kinds of planters and arrangements of pots and other containers

A white brugmansia dominates the corner of a porch and a front garden

that inspire creativity. Fountains made of many different materials, old and new, grace walls and gardens. Quite a few restaurants, hotels, and museums in the Historic District have pretty courtyard gardens or larger ones for their guests to enjoy. The courtyard of the Mills House Hotel is paved in a highly decorative pattern that was designed by Loutrel Briggs and meant to be viewed from above. Some pretty gardens in the city have owners who run bed-and-breakfast establishments or small inns. One dress shop used to have fashion shows in a courtyard full of azaleas behind its establishment on King Street.

Topiaries, window boxes, and a fine stone carriage block decorate a handsome Legare Street entrance.

There are receptions in the beautifully maintained sculpture garden of an art dealer on Church Street, and the outdoor furniture room of the Historic Charleston Foundation shop on Meeting Street is in an open courtyard where weary tourists often stop to rest. There are charming gardens leading to artists' studios and alleys that are happily tended by groups of neighbors and even the occasional parking lot that is well-planted. Charleston is truly a city of gardens.

Appendix

FIFTY-TWO WEEKS OF BLOOM

Bright flowers in window boxes on Tradd Street are in full bloom in July.

Jan MacDougal, a well-known and loved local horticulturist, botanical research consultant, master gardener, flower arranger, and show judge (with other notable talents), wrote a charming and informative booklet for Historic Charleston Foundation. In *Charleston in Bloom,* she describes thirty-two blooming plants seen often in Charleston gardens, gives a timeline for their approximate blooming period, and shows them in stunning flower arrangements.

Inspired by her publication, I kept a journal for part of 2012, all of 2013, and part of 2014 on the trees, shrubs, bulbs, and perennials I noted were in bloom in the city. Mrs. MacDougal divided her booklet into early-, mid-, and late-season categories, but I have not been as precise. We had a warm winter and an unusually long and cool spring in 2013 with very little frost, so some

Cassia corymbosa tumbles over a wall on Legare Street.

of the entries given below are a bit surprising. Common names are used as often as possible, and the list is not all-inclusive by any means.

Some years are, of course, much more floriferous than others. I cannot recall a summer of more gorgeous crape myrtles than in 2013. There have been years, such as 1972, when a warm winter and early spring coincided for a knockout late-February show, or 1979, when it snowed in March. After Hurricane Hugo in September 1989 the leaves were ripped from the trees and shrubs, resulting in odd bloom times over the next few seasons. I have purposely omitted most annuals and a long list of tropicals, as these tender imports are frequently grown in microclimates or protected during very cold weather.

DECEMBER, JANUARY, AND FEBRUARY (our winter months)

Azaleas
Camellias
Iris
Lady Banks rose
Magnolias (saucer and tulip)
Narcissus
Noisette roses
Poinsettias
Quinces
Redbud trees (*Cercis canadensis*)
Roses
Sasanquas
Sea myrtle (also called she-muckle by locals)
Shower tree (*Cassia corymbosa*)
Snowdrops (*Leucojum aestivum*)
Tea olives
Wand flower (*Gaura)*

MARCH, APRIL, AND MAY (our spring months)

Abelia
Agave
Amaryllis
Atamasco lilies (naked ladies)
Azaleas, southern hybrid and native
Banana shrub (*Michelia figo*)
Bottlebrush (*Callistemon rigidus*)
Carolina jessamine (state flower of South Carolina)
Cassia
Cherry trees, Yoshino and Kwanzan
Chinese flame tree (*Koelreuteria bipinnata*)
Chinese fringe flower (*Loropetalum*)
Clematis
Coreopsis
Crabapple
Crinum lilies
Cross vine
Daffodils
Dogwood
Echinacea
Fern, Cinnamon
Gaillardia
Gladiolus (magenta Byzantine glad)
Globe flower (gomphrena)
Hollies
Honeysuckle
Indian hawthorn
Iris
Jasmine, Confederate
Lady Banks rose, yellow and white
Larkspur (self-seeding annual)
Ligustrum (privet)
Oleander
Peach trees, white and peppermint
Pear trees
Pittosporum
Roses
Spiraea (bridal-wreath)
Spiderworts
Tung oil tree
Wisteria

Clematis blooming on a garden swing

JUNE, JULY, AND AUGUST (our summer months, although September can be very warm)

Agapanthus (lily of the Nile), blue and white
Althea (purple)
Caladiums
Cannas
Coral vine
Crape myrtles
Crinum lilies

Gardenia
Geranium (hardy)
Ginger lilies
Golden rain tree (*Koelreuteria paniculata*)
Hibiscus
Honeysuckle vine (common)
Hydrangeas
Lantana
Lilies (oriental)
Magnolia (southern)
Mimosa
Parkinsonia (Jerusalem thorn tree)
Pomegranate
Roses
Ruellia (Mexican petunia, breakfast plant)
Salvias
Shrimp plant
Spider lilies
Trumpet vines, orange and yellow
Vitex (chaste tree)

Magnolia blossoms on the tree in front of the Nathaniel Russell House

SEPTEMBER, OCTOBER, AND NOVEMBER (our fall months, when many summer plants are still blooming)

Camellias
Datura
Chrysanthemums
Roses
Sasanquas
Swamp daisy (*Helianthus angustifolius*)
Tea olive

A Datura plant in a West Ashley garden

Sources for Further Reading

Bailey, L. H. *Hortus Third*. New York: Macmillan, 1976.

Briggs, Loutrel W. *Charleston Gardens*. Columbia: University of South Carolina Press, 1951.

Cameron, Louisa Pringle. *The Private Gardens of Charleston*. Columbia: University of South Carolina Press, 1992.

———. *The Secret Gardens of Charleston*. Columbia: University of South Carolina Press, 2001.

Chibbaro, Anthony. *Images of America: The Charleston Exposition*. Mt. Pleasant, S.C.: Arcadia Publishing, 2001.

Côté, Richard N. *Mary's World: Love, War, and Family Ties in Nineteenth-Century Charleston*. Mt. Pleasant, S.C.: Corinthian Books, 2001.

Cothran, James R. *Charleston Gardens and the Landscape Legacy of Loutrel Briggs*. Columbia: University of South Carolina Press, 2010.

———. *Gardens and Historic Plants of the Antebellum South*. Columbia: University of South Carolina Press, 2003.

———. *Gardens of Historic Charleston*. Columbia: University of South Carolina Press, 1995.

Eberle, Kevin R. *A History of Charleston's Hampton Park*. Charleston: History Press, 2012.

Foote, Leonard E., and Samuel B. Jones Jr. *Native Shrubs and Woody Vines of the Southeast: Landscaping Uses and Identification*. Portland, Ore.: Timber Press, 1989.

Garden Club of Charleston. *The Gardeners' Guide for Charleston and the Lowcountry*. Charleston, 1990.

Garten, P. J., and Brian F. Smith. *Some Like It Hot: Plants That Thrive in Hot and Humid Weather*. Charleston: Wyrick, 2004.

Halfacre, R. Gordon, and Anne R. Shawcroft. *Landscape Plants of the Southeast*. Raleigh: Sparks Press, 1989.

Leighton, Ann. *American Gardens in the Eighteenth Century "For Use or for Delight"*. Amherst: University of Massachusetts Press, 1976.

MacDonald, John W., Jr. *McBee House: A Narrative Tour Conducted by Ian MacDonald*. Charleston: Ashley Hall, 2004.

MacDougal, Jan. *Charleston in Bloom*. Charleston: Oak Manor Press, 1991.

Phillips, Ted Ashton, Jr. *City of the Silent: The Charlestonians of Magnolia Cemetery*. Columbia: University of South Carolina Press, 2010.

Poston, Jonathan H. *The Buildings of Charleston*. Columbia: University of South Carolina Press, 1997.

Ripley, Warren. *The Battery: Charleston, South Carolina*. Charleston: Evening Post Publishing, 1977.

Schenk, George. *The Complete Shade Gardener.* Boston: Houghton Mifflin Company, 1984.

Strauch, Ileana. *Ashley Hall*. Charleston: Arcadia Publishing, 2003.

Trustees' Garden Club. *Garden Guide to the Lower South*. Savannah,1986.

Waring, Laura Witte. *The Way It Was in Charleston as Recalled by Laura Witte Waring*. Charleston: Evening Post Publishing, 2010.

Annuals and perennials cascade from a window box on an historic home.
The round plaque is a Carolopolis Award from the Preservation Society.

Index

Page numbers given in *italic* type indicate illustrations.